GW00901999

Journey into the Unknown

Wolfgang Pietrek

Design © 131 Design Ltd
www.131design.org
Text © Wolfgang Pietrek
www.wolfgangpietrek.com

ISBN 978-1-912821-16-7
Published 2016 by Tricorn Books 131 High
Street, Old Portsmouth PO1 2HW
www.tricornbooks.co.uk
Printed & bound in UK

Contents

To my wife Elaine
and our sons
Nicholas and Christopher
and their families

Introduction

If we were given the capability of foreseeing the future would we in the end have the courage and self-belief to expose ourselves to the vagaries on the road ahead?

Some individuals readily adopt the fatalistic outlook that their future is shaped by divine providence and accept the ups and downs in dignified submission.

Others, and I think a considerable majority of us, have the belief or maybe the illusion, that what we see in the crystal ball is merely a mirage of future events and that a strong will, determination or even patience can at least influence our final destination.

Since I never attempted to gaze into a crystal ball on that historic day in April 1957 when crossing the Channel for the first time, I deprived myself of what would have been a most exhilarating and eventful experience. But had I tried to take a glimpse at the future I can only say that I would not have attempted to manipulate it in any way whatsoever.

At the beginning, it truly was a journey into the unknown, to a land in which the horrors of destruction and the pain of personal losses were still vividly remembered.

And yet the hand of reconciliation showed itself already when the friendly border control official in Dover, when stamping my passport and reading the letter from the Coats Company in Glasgow, welcomed me with the prophetic words, "You still have a long way to go. Have a good journey and good luck."

And these prophetic words became the beginning of a

journey which not only widened my own personal horizon, but which after many years of testing my patience to its limit was now finally progressing towards its conclusion. Or maybe not!

Finally, with my car safely inside the ferry and the gaping hole at the rear being closed by a huge iron gate, another milestone of my journey was left behind. Although I knew my terrestrial destination, I still could not completely shed the feeling of yet another journey into the unknown. What did the crystal ball have in store for me? Again, I shall give it a miss.

Chapter 1

Welcome Joseph. I am glad to see you again. It must be about a year since you were last here. And look at the changes which have occurred in such a short time. New roads and houses have left very little of the old rural environment and the tranquillity which I had treasured so much. All our objections were simply brushed aside and we ended up being accused of being old-fashioned and insensitive to the needs of a modern society.

Maybe there is a little truth in that, Wolfgang. The needs of our modern society are very different from the post-war years which must have influenced your outlook and by necessity concentrated on reconstruction or Wiederaufbau *as you called it. What is happening around you now is commonly described as 'Progress' and you must admit it brings with it many advantages also for you.*

You are right, Joseph. The past is for reminiscing and today is for accepting and dealing with new challenges.

Now make yourself comfortable, Joseph, while I fetch the apple strudel and the bottle of Alsace Riesling, which I said at our last encounter we would share again over my recollections of yet another border crossing and my ensuing journey into the unknown.

Well, that sounds absolutely perfect and I look forward with great anticipation to hear how your new host country received you. If I remember correctly, it was April 1957 when you left your adopted home town of Freiburg and headed for the port of Calais for your Channel crossing to Dover.

Yes, Joseph, it must have been about mid-morning when the train reached the eastern outskirts of Calais. The speed almost reduced to a crawl and very soon, with the brakes causing a slight shudder of the coach, the train finally came to a halt in the harbour station of Calais.

A few porters walked casually along the platform, but with waving hands appearing from opened coach windows and doors, all of them found themselves hired very quickly. Loudspeakers announced in French and English how to proceed to the waiting ferry. I suppose it was too much to expect for these announcements also to be given in German.

As an able-bodied 23-year-old I regarded the hiring of a porter a bit over the top, particularly since unlike most of the other travellers, I only had one suitcase plus a small cotton bag with my books, travel documents and my German newspaper.

We were directed to walk down a rather narrow, long platform towards the tail end of the train. A group of English soldiers emerged from the last coach. Since the British Zone of Occupation was in the north of Germany, their coach was probably added to our train during a stop en route to Calais. They sounded a very happy lot, undeterred by the no-nonsense voice of their commanding officer who was probably telling them to form an orderly line.

As I walked down the station platform, I could already see to my left the berthed ferry which did not look any bigger than the train ferry, which in my early childhood days I had often watched sailing out of Warnemüende to Gedser in Denmark.

I was directed to one of the two gangways leading up to the ferry and after having my boarding papers checked I found myself once again on a British means of transport. The ferry looked very well cared for as if it had been repainted just recently. A large poster in a corridor informed me that the ship was called *Halladale*, operated by the Townsend Channel Ferries Company. A framed notice next to the poster described the history of this ship and with the help of my pocket dictionary I discovered that she was launched on the River Clyde in Glasgow as recently as 1944 and not as a ferry but as a warship. Maybe she was part of the big armada at the D-Day landings in France during that year. She must have gone through a very comprehensive conversion to serve now as an elegant-looking ferry to shuttle between France and England.

The main corridor led straight to a comfortable-looking salon with chairs and tables right at the front of the ship. The windows seemed rather small, but still big enough to provide a good all-round view. It soon became obvious that this part of the ship was favoured by several of the passengers, as the chairs and tables were quickly occupied by my fellow travellers.

Since I had heard so much about the magical white cliffs

of Dover I was determined to secure myself a seat near one of the front windows to get the best possible view on our approach to Dover. The chairs and table next to me were taken up by three adults whose language I could not make out, but I guessed they were from Czechoslovakia.

A little distance away from me I noticed a single gentleman sitting at a table unfurling a German newspaper. It gave me quite a feeling of comfort to know that there was at least one fellow countryman on board, although I did not think it appropriate to make myself known to him.

A shrill whistle sound and a vibration throughout the whole ship indicated that we were about to commence our voyage to Dover.

It all sounds very comfortable and organised compared with the border crossings you did in your teenage years. Now, being an adult did you still have that feeling of adventure and anxiety when stepping into the unknown?

It is difficult to answer this one, Joseph. I certainly looked upon this journey as an adventure, but the thrill of the forbidden crossing was missing. Here I was, a young adult and a bundle of documents, papers and money in my cotton bag which would ensure that I could safely reach my final destination. And yet, I could not entirely rid myself of a nagging thought. Had I been too hasty in accepting this challenging assignment? Why had the Coats Company in Glasgow decided to seek out a young German to come to Scotland for what had loosely been described as 'career advancement'?

On reflection, I should have asked at the interview in Freiburg as to what would happen after completing my training period in Scotland, but during the encounter in the Freiburg boardroom I was clearly too overwhelmed to raise this vital question. I admit that all of a sudden I felt a little unsure of myself. But what choice did I have now, with the ferry just passing the pier head of Calais harbour?

I suddenly remembered an occurrence way back, when as a youngster I nearly abandoned a crossing of the Iron Curtain, had it not been for the encouraging words of a friendly farmer who said something like, "Well young man, you have covered nearly half the distance, you might as well finish the job."

It took me a little while to remove these thoughts from my mind and finally I decided to engage in a practical experiment by purchasing a cup of coffee at a bar at the rear of this salon. Handing over my £1 note, my change consisted of an array of different coins plus a buff-looking note for 10 shillings. All this was most welcome as I now had the opportunity to familiarise myself more thoroughly with this strange non-metric coinage system

I have to admit, Joseph, it took me several months before I really felt comfortable with pounds, shillings and pence, and initially, when making purchases, I merely kept trusting the seller would give me the correct change. To my horror, I also discovered on the ferry that all measurements and weights were expressed in strange-sounding non-metric units. I had already learnt that unlike everybody else in Europe, the English drove their cars on the left side of the road, but what else lay in store for me?

Time slipped by very quickly. The sea was calm and it must have been just over the hour when suddenly several passengers from the centre of the salon made their way towards the windows at the front and right-hand side as the white cliffs appeared in full view. I had seen pictures of them before in a magazine, but here they were right before my eyes. It truly was a spectacle.

The entry into Dover harbour was equally impressive. Judging by the number of piers and buildings, this clearly was a main gateway between England and the Continent and I could imagine that this port must have played a leading part in the widely publicised evacuation of British and French troops from Dunkirk in 1940.

We swiftly disembarked on a comfortable, wide gangway. Out of nowhere the soldiers appeared again and I saw them heading towards what looked like a military transporter on the side of this large, impressive Dover Marine Station building. I joined a queue of passengers to present my passport with the visa entry plus a letter from the Coats Company in Glasgow which stated the reason for my journey. All I was hoping for now was that the border control official would not ask me too many questions which would then expose my limited command of the English language. When I reached the desk, the officer gave me a friendly smile and after having read the Company letter and having stamped my passport he said, "You have still got a long way to go, sir. Have a good journey and good luck." I was quite chuffed to be addressed as 'sir'.

According to the list of instructions I had received in Freiburg I was now to buy a one-way ticket from the Dover Marine Station to Victoria Station in London and thereafter proceed by taxi to a hotel near Euston Station. I think the hotel was called the Corah Hotel which as it turned out was within walking distance from the station.

The Dover Marine Station was a massive building, much larger than the Harbour Station in Calais. The purchase of the train ticket was again a transaction based entirely on trust. After having handed over a £5 note and not having understood the counter clerk when stating the ticket price to me, I simply grabbed the change and moved quickly to one side to let the next passenger make her purchase.

Did the reception so far remove any of the doubts and anxieties which had troubled you whilst on the ferry boat?

Yes, the friendly and trouble-free passage through the passport control and the ease of transfer from ferry to train made me feel more confident again. In fact, I was now reaching a stage again where my anxiety was replaced by a form of curiosity as to what this country had in store for me.

Victoria Station turned out to be a huge rail terminal and reminded me of the large inner city stations in Frankfurt and Munich. The station was buzzing with people and long queues were forming outside at the taxi ranks. The black London taxis were yet another new experience. They pulled up in large numbers, discharging their passengers at the station and they quickly reduced the length of the queue of waiting travellers. I was truly impressed by the efficiency of it all.

When my turn came I simply showed the driver the letter of reservation for my hotel and with a nod of his head and a laconic "OK" we set off on my first journey through London. After a minute or so from leaving the station the driver suddenly shouted with a clear voice. "Parliament Square and Westminster Palace ahead!" Pressing my face against the taxi window, I could not only take in the full width of this imposing building but also got a good glimpse of the famous Big Ben tower. It all was a sight to behold. And when a few minutes later the driver shouted "Trafalgar Square" I became so enthralled by it all that I was hoping that the location of my hotel would be a good distance away so that I could savour more of this magnificent metropolis.

I would imagine that from your school days, and also films and the media, you were familiar with some of the iconic landmarks of this remarkable city.

Yes, I was, Joseph, but seeing it all now with my own eyes was quite a different thing. Strangely enough it was during my school years in communist East Germany that London emerged as a place of special interest in our history classes. Not only was it hailed as the city where Karl Marx published his first edition of *Das Kapital* in 1867, but it was also the historic place where in 1903 Lenin laid the foundation for the Bolshevik movement, which, as we all know, changed the political landscape in Europe and beyond.

As I was being driven along these streets with magnificent buildings on either side, they almost radiated the words 'Empire' and 'Power' to me. It made me wonder how such a nation could simultaneously tolerate and cope with the emergence of such reactionary ideas and movements on its own home ground. Would this demonstration of tolerance also extend to people who not so long ago were their dreaded enemy? Maybe the smile on the face of the immigration officer in Dover was a good omen.

The taxi driver shouted out a few more names as we travelled along but they did not register with me. I had hoped to hear the name 'Buckingham Palace' but it never came. I was fully absorbed in watching the traffic and buildings when suddenly the taxi stopped outside the Corah Hotel. I had reached my destination.

I handed the driver a £5 note and again relied on his honesty for my change. He seemed very pleased when I handed him one of those buff 10 shilling notes as a tip. I learnt later that that was very generous.

The receptionist was a young lady who spoke with a very different accent from the taxi driver. As it turned out she was from Belfast, but to my surprise and relief she could converse in French, which at this stage was still the easiest way for me to make myself understood. When I handed over my passport and the letter of reservation she must have noticed that the booking originated from J. & P. Coats in Glasgow.

"This is a very well-known company," she said. "An uncle of mine works for them in Paisley in one of their big mills. Are they also your employer?"

Somehow I managed, in stuttering French, to explain to her the reason for my journey to Glasgow, at the end of which she said that she had a very nice room for me at the front of the hotel. When she handed me various leaflets, one of them showing the enormous London Underground network, and others promoting museums and cultural events, I told her that I would very much like to see Buckingham Palace and also the Tower of London before departing on my midday train to Scotland.

"There is a lot more to London than those two places," she said in her strongly accented French, "but I will organise a taxi for you in the morning for a sightseeing tour of London and we shall tell the driver to take you in good time to Euston Station for your departure to Glasgow." I was quite taken aback by so much friendliness.

An additional surprise was when she said that according to the letter of reservation the hotel was to bill J. & P. Coats for all the costs incurred at the hotel.

My wallet was still well filled with green and blue banknotes and when the receptionist gave me an indication of the likely cost of the train ticket to Glasgow I felt confident that I could easily afford the luxury of a London sightseeing tour by taxi.

Once again I must say, luck and good fortune seems to follow you even on your journey into the unknown. Only a short while ago, on the ferry boat from Calais, you told me that you were plagued by a feeling of doubt about the whole venture and now, here you are planning to conquer London in a morning.

Yes, all of a sudden my past fears and questions during the ferry passage were replaced by a feeling of a new adventure with different challenges. It lacked the thrill and dangers of my Iron Curtain border crossings in my younger days, but nevertheless it now became my new, all absorbing leitmotiv.

My room turned out to be very spacious and elegantly furnished, but lacked one vital gadget – a telephone. On my arrival at the hotel I had already noticed two cabins in the foyer which looked like telephone boxes. And that is what they were.

With the help of the friendly receptionist from Belfast, I managed to get a connection to my parents in Freiburg who were audibly pleased to hear about my safe arrival in London. As to be expected, my mother bombarded me with questions about the train journey, the crossing from Calais to Dover and many more to which I summarily responded that I would cover it all in a letter once I reached my final destination in Scotland. Over the years, it became well known to – and grudgingly accepted by – members of my family that I did not give frequent running commentaries of my travels and movements, an attitude which in later years invited also strong criticism from my own wife.

After my telephone call to Freiburg I decided to go for a walk with the main purpose of finding out how near or far it is to Euston Station. It was only a very short walk and whilst there I checked out the location of the ticket offices where the following day I would be buying my ticket to Glasgow. On my return to the hotel another pleasant surprise awaited me. The friendly receptionist gave me a piece of paper, which she said contained instructions for the taxi driver whom she had booked to pick me up in the morning for my sightseeing tour and final delivery to the railway station.

"Go for the early breakfast," she said, "and be ready for your departure by half past nine."

I must say, Wolfgang, London has certainly received you with open arms. From what you tell me, it seems that Irish lady has probably taken a shine to you.

Yes, I began to think that myself.

When, after a good night's rest I started on my programme for the day, I was deeply disappointed when a young man seemed to be in charge of the reception counter. The Irish lady, I was told, would resume work again in the afternoon. I really would have liked to express my personal thanks to her for having given me such a pleasant welcome to England. Even her choice of taxi for my tour of London showed her thoughtfulness. When, after having retrieved my passport, I stepped outside the hotel, the young taxi driver grabbed my suitcase and with a big smile on his face opened the cab door for me. For a moment I thought that the Irish lady might even have managed to find a taxi driver who could speak German or French, but clearly that was too much to expect. When the young man finally addressed me, he spoke in English but very slowly and he used simple words, probably the way English parents speak to their young children. He said that he had been instructed by a lady from the hotel to speak to me in this manner. In addition, he said, he had received a list of London landmarks which were a 'must' on this tour, plus the time when I had to be discharged at Euston Station. The whole organisation of my trip seemed flawless.

I enjoyed every minute of the ensuing grand tour of London and I was particularly pleased about the fact that I was able to follow the driver's running commentary, which he conducted throughout at slow speed and with simple sentences.

Having read and heard so much about the wartime devastation inflicted upon this city I still expected to see some evidence of that, but apart from a gap here and there in the rows of buildings, the occasional sight of a crane or sites shielded off with wooden fencing, the post-war reconstruction appeared equally impressive to what I had seen in Munich or the villages and towns in France which I had toured only recently.

When we finally reached Euston Station I really felt that I was very fortunate to have seen so much of this truly imperial metropolis. Little did I know at this stage that 16 years later I would be working in London for one of Britain's largest companies.

I thanked the young taxi driver for letting me share with him this informative tour of his own home town and especially for communicating everything to me in such a simple and nearly fully understandable manner. It is amazing how this relatively short experience raised my confidence significantly and I felt that I would probably be mastering this language in the not-too-distant future.

Ever since arriving in Dover it had struck me that whenever a crowd of people were trying to obtain a service at a street kiosk, or board a bus or, as here at the railway station, were trying to buy a railway ticket, they always tended to form a queue. This was much more civilised, or shall I say orderly, than the often-seen push and shove of crowds in Continental countries. I also noticed that in the queue I had joined here in the huge station hall, several gentlemen were donning a black, almost helmet-shaped headgear which only a few days later was also to become part of my personal outfit. It was a bowler hat which I have retained to this very day.

When I asked the ticket clerk for a one-way ticket to Glasgow, I had problems in understanding him clearly behind the glass screen when he mentioned the price to me. I clearly was not the first foreigner he had to deal with and to quickly complete the transaction he wrote the price on a piece of paper.

The whole station was a massive building, once again an end of line station and, although not as large as the ones in Frankfurt or Munich, it had an impressive number of platforms.

I walked along a few coaches to see if I could find an empty compartment, but it appeared that this was quite a popular train for people travelling north. Halfway up the train I found a compartment which was occupied by one middle-aged lady. Upon entering the compartment with my suitcase and cotton bag she gave me a curious look and my "Good day!" greeting was only met with a muttering from her which I did not understand. I settled in at the farthest point from her in the compartment, as I gathered from her facial expression that she would have preferred the whole compartment to herself. In a way, this suited me quite well as it saved me from having to make polite conversation with my rudimentary English.

As the train finally pulled out of the station, we were still the only two people in this compartment.

The sprawling suburban areas seemed to stretch over many kilometres before we reached the more open countryside which still appeared dotted with clusters of houses and also quaint-looking villages.

I was about to get my English phrase book out to learn a few new words and sentences, when my fellow passenger suddenly addressed me. She pointed at the suitcase just by her feet and, by pointing upwards to the luggage rack and muttering a few words, it did not require much guessing that she was asking me to lift her suitcase up into the rack above her.

I willingly obliged, but even after my service I was merely rewarded with a rather stony "Thank you" and her face continued to show that any further social contact with this intruding young man would be avoided.

I specifically mention this experience on the train, because ever since my recent arrival in Britain, I had encountered friendly people with smiles on their faces. Maybe this lady had just suffered some bereavement and was on her way to a funeral? Or had she spotted my German newspaper which on my arrival in the compartment I had laid out next to my seat? Whatever the reason, as the train sped through the countryside she immersed herself in a book and I continued with my phrase book and also watched the landscape flying past.

With about five hours of travelling time ahead of me, I was wondering if my fellow traveller would also be going all the way to Glasgow or leaving the train at one of the many stopping points on our way up north.

It was already late afternoon when she suddenly addressed me again and pointed up to her suitcase which she wanted to be brought down. Having done so I expected once more a curt 'Thank you' but no, this time she put on a rather solemn voice and, although I could not make out every word, I think I got the gist of it.

From my openly displayed *Frankfurter Allgemeine* newspaper, she had clearly come to the conclusion from the outset that I was German. What I think she tried to convey to me now was that the Germans had caused her so much suffering and hardship in the past that she found it hard to strike up a friendly conversation with any one of them. Even now, with the war having ended so many years ago. Somehow I managed to make out that she had not only had her home destroyed during one of the bombing raids on London, but even more tragically her husband had been killed during the evacuation from Dunkirk.

How does one respond to that in any language? Even if I had had a good command of English would

22

there have been any point in explaining to her that her fate was shared by millions of ordinary people on both sides of the conflict. I would have liked to tell her how my generation had taken their elders to task over the gruesome events during those years and that we now try our hardest to build new bridges between former combatants. I probably would have reminded her also that the firestorms of Dresden and Hamburg had left equally deep scars in Germany.

I can see that you must have understood enough to find yourself face to face with a rather emotional issue which, I suppose, you must have expected to encounter sooner or later anyway.

This is correct, Joseph, but the smile of the Dover immigration officer, the friendly reception at the London Hotel and the helpfulness of that young London taxi driver must have dimmed my awareness of the traumas which many people of this country had endured during the war years. On reflection, I thought, my fellow passenger had probably rendered me a very useful service by bringing me back to earth with her outpourings.

I simply stood there, short of words, when she picked up her suitcase and probably forcing herself to say a brief "Goodbye" she readied herself to leave the train which had just come to a halt in a town called Carlisle.

For the rest of my journey I found it hard to stop thinking about this encounter. Would I have to face repeats of this kind amongst the staff in the Coats Company? After all, Glasgow, as I had read somewhere, had also suffered from heavy German air raids and Scottish regiments had been involved in many of the fiercest battles of the war.

With daylight fading, the countryside outside became less clear but that did not disguise the fact that we were now getting into a decidedly mountainous region. I quite enjoyed having the whole compartment to myself, but all too soon houses and industrial buildings appeared on either side of the train. We were on our final approach to Glasgow.

Finally, with the speed almost reduced to a crawl, the train entered the huge Central Station of Glasgow. Who would be there to meet me?

People were quickly emerging from the coaches, all streaming towards the exit gates. Once on the platform myself and having put my German newspaper under my left arm as instructed, I stood still, trying to identify a person who was stationary or even walking against the stream upwards on the platform. No sign of anybody.

Rather disappointed I followed the stream of passengers towards the gates. As I approached them I noticed a tall young man standing on the other side who clearly had his eyes fixed on the emerging travellers.

He must have spotted my newspaper from a distance because he suddenly started waving to me. I have to admit, I was very relieved at that moment. I was even more relieved that, when we finally shook hands, he greeted me with *"Willkommen in Schottland, Wolfgang. Mein Name ist Andrew."*

When he continued to ask me in perfect German what sort of a journey I had had, I knew I was in safe hands. I suddenly remembered the reassuring parting shot from Dr Mez in Freiburg, when I voiced my concern about my limited knowledge of the English language. "That is only a minor obstacle," he replied. "The people in Glasgow will look after you."

Such a reception must have removed any of the anxieties you may still have harboured, particularly after your unsavoury encounter with your fellow traveller only a little while earlier.

Yes, Joseph, even my suitcase suddenly felt a lot lighter. With all linguistic barriers removed, I firstly complimented Andrew on his excellent German and whilst walking along the concourse to a ticket counter and finally to another platform I had extracted quite a lot of information out of him.

He was a year older than me and originated from Edinburgh where he had also studied modern languages, in his case German and French. Immediately after his studies he had spent some time in France but he said he had never set foot in Germany. After his sojourn in France, Andrew responded to an advertisement by J. & P. Coats who were looking for university graduates to join their management training scheme for senior positions in their worldwide organisation. The lure of the wider world was enough for Andrew to apply. And here he was now, receiving a fellow trainee from Germany on whom he could test out his linguistic skills.

The German Language Department at Edinburgh University must have had very competent tutors because Andrew's pronunciation and grammar were virtually flawless.

It struck me only a few months later that Scottish people in general had fewer problems in coping with some of the more guttural German words compared with the English.

The train was decidedly less comfortable than the London to Glasgow train, but then this was also only a short-distance journey.

"At this hour we at least get a seat," Andrew said. "As you will shortly find out, during the rush hour it is sometimes difficult to even get onto this train."

After only a few stops, Andrew gestured to me to get ready to leave the train at the next station. The town was called Paisley.

Once outside the station, Andrew hailed one of the waiting taxis, which unlike in London, were ordinary saloon cars. Just a minute or so into our journey Andrew drew my attention to a block of tall, brick buildings.

"These are some of the Coats Mills here in Paisley," he said, "and from what I have read in our training programme, we are all expected to spend a few weeks in there to do hands-on work."

The mills looked gigantic compared with the factory buildings back in Freiburg. Seeing all this here now in Scotland reinforced my already held impression that I was part of a very large enterprise.

After a short journey we reached our final destination, a large house with its own spacious curved driveway. This was Makerston House, the Company-owned residence for their management trainees.

I was greeted by a middle-aged lady, the resident matron and manageress, and a bevy of young men of about my own age with curiosity written all over their faces as to who this newcomer might be. I am sure that prior to being sent off to Glasgow to meet me Andrew would have let it be known that the new arrival came from Germany, but he clearly did not tell anyone that I had only a limited knowledge of the English language. With Andrew's help, I introduced myself to all my future colleagues. The majority of them were either Scottish or English but there were also two from far away Brazil and Chile, and two from Spain and Switzerland. Now Germany became the latest addition to that international list.

Andrew quickly showed me my room which was sparsely furnished but with a very comfortable-looking bed.

"Do not unpack now," he said, "because a late supper has been laid out for all of us and there will also be a round of drinks from our house bar to celebrate your arrival."

With Andrew constantly by my side, it soon turned into a lively multi-lingual welcome party as I could readily converse with my new colleague from Switzerland and could also try out my rusty Spanish on my fellow trainees from Spain and Chile. The final, almost ceremonial act of the evening was the addition of my name to the list in the house bar where each individual's consumption of alcoholic drinks was recorded for settlement at the end of each month.

Before retiring to my room, Andrew took me aside to explain the Makerston House rules and also the proceedings for the next day. The most welcome piece of news was when he said that he had been given the task of being my personal guardian and translator during the initial phases of our training programme.

"Tomorrow morning we are expected at the headquarter offices in Glasgow," he added, "which means an early start to the day as it is a good 20-minute walk to the station."

I thought to myself, the gloves have come off very quickly. No more taxis at the Company's expense.

Chapter 2

After what had been a truly eventful day I slept very soundly and if Andrew had not knocked on my door in the morning, I would have been in trouble on my very first day.

My first Scottish breakfast was another new experience, but merely one in a long row of more to come. When staying at the London Hotel I had already noticed people with a variety of cooked foods on their breakfast plates, but here now I really came face to face with it. Bacon and fried eggs, sausages plus cooked tomatoes and even a helping of scrambled egg. And if this was not enough, there was also an endless supply of toast and marmalade. It was certainly a novel way to start the day and contrasted significantly with my usual *Broetchen*, butter and jam plus a cup of coffee back home.

The next surprise was not long in waiting. When Andrew finally emerged from his room he was adorned with the same strangely shaped headgear I had noticed on those gentlemen at Euston Station. The bowler hat.

As we started off on our walk to the station, Andrew explained to me that aspiring young managers like ourselves were expected to observe a certain sartorial code and wearing a bowler hat when working at or visiting the Company's Head Office was part of this code.

I had to admit it looked very smart on Andrew and it certainly made him appear even taller. Being of a smaller stature it occurred to me that such a hat would easily add a few centimetres to my own overall posture. Andrew promised me that on the coming Saturday he would take me to a large Paisley department store for me to purchase such a piece of headgear.

No doubt you had to acquire also the proverbial English umbrella to complete your new dress code?

Yes, Joseph, you are right. Although not really part of the dress code, I was advised to also purchase an umbrella, but for purely practical reasons as I was soon to find out.

Having spent most of my travel fund already on my sightseeing tour of London and the railway journey to Glasgow, I intimated to Andrew that at this moment I probably could not afford to pay for these purchases. However, Andrew quickly put my mind at rest by informing me that I would be getting a special settling-in allowance plus a weekly sum to cover my future sundry expenses and train fares to Glasgow. With a grin on his face he added that for most of the 'Makerstonians' a large portion of the allowance is needed to settle the monthly bill from the house bar.

On our brisk walk to the station I gained my first impression of Paisley town centre and its mixture of grey and reddish-looking stone buildings. Now, in full daylight I also got a clearer view of the large complex of buildings making up the Coats Mills in close proximity to the ancient Abbey of Paisley. By the time we reached the station I was convinced that this town, although so very different from places I had previously lived in, would also offer interesting and stimulating experiences.

The train journey to Glasgow was uneventful except that we shared the compartment with a youngish looking gentleman, dressed in a smart-looking jacket and a kilt. I had seen pictures of kilted Scotsmen before but this was my first real life encounter.

The Coats headquarters were only a short distance away from Central Station. It was a large reddish sandstone building. The rather modest-looking main entrance door betrayed somehow the world-embracing activities which were conducted on the five floors of this building, as I was to find out in the days to come. Several people entered the building with us, but they quickly disappeared into a maze of offices on the ground floor.

For Andrew, this was already his third visit to the headquarters and the gentleman at the reception desk recognised him immediately. We were asked to wait a moment and, after a brief telephone call, Andrew was told to proceed with me to the office of the personnel manager, the location of which he clearly remembered from his earlier visit.

My mind went back to our rather forbidding personnel manager back in the Freiburg offices. Would I now have to face an equally intimidating character?

As the door opened and I saw the gentleman I felt

immediately that this was a friendly and caring individual. He did not look very much older than we were and with a cheerful voice he welcomed me to Scotland.

"My name is Robin," he said, "and I am the Company training manager. I speak no German, but with Andrew by your side you are in safe hands, but make sure he also teaches you English quickly."

Within one hour all administrative issues were cleared up, I received my settling-in allowance and was also informed about my weekly allowance which would be made available each Friday at Makerston House. Finally, Andrew and I were given our training programme for the next three weeks which consisted of jointly visiting a series of departments in this building, starting the following Monday.

After an extensive tour around the building and Robin having explained to several individuals that they would be seeing more of Andrew and myself in the weeks to come, we finally ended up in the office of the overseas director whose portfolio of countries also included Germany. Again, a very welcoming reception and after a few questions about my journey from Freiburg to Scotland and wishing me all the best for my training course, we were dismissed.

All this must surely have exceeded your expectations. By the hour, it seems to become less and less a journey into the unknown.

I agree, Joseph, it is rapidly turning into a journey of pleasant discoveries.

We finally travelled back to Paisley, avoiding the rush

hour and once in Paisley we walked just a short distance to a large department store where in a well-stocked men's outfit department we bought a bowler hat, which I think I mentioned before, has stayed with me to this day. And standing beside Andrew now it certainly added a few centimetres to my height. With the subsequent purchase of an umbrella I now felt ready to face the challenges ahead.

Once back at Makerston House, I retired to my room and wrote the overdue letter to my parents, which I had promised them after my rather short telephone call from the hotel in London. I also wrote a short note to Dr Mez informing him that he was absolutely right when he had reassured me that "the people in Glasgow will look after you."

Throughout these very first days, as indeed in the weeks to come, Andrew was not merely acting as an interpreter but he was pushing me hard to repeat long sentences in English, corrected my mistakes and helped me admirably to adapt myself to my new Scottish environment. I wondered sometimes if in the reverse situation I would have had the patience to 'shadow' someone during all my waking hours and forego quite a number of my own private interests, as Andrew clearly must have done.

Our training programme at the Glasgow Head Office was covering a wide range of different departments. It made me even more aware of the international spread of the Coats 'Empire', covering all five continents and with factories dotted all over the globe. Who would have thought that a simple cotton thread could form the bedrock for such a massive enterprise?

One day, on a journey back from Glasgow, Andrew mentioned to me that the Modern Language Department at Edinburgh University had used foreign language films in their tuition programmes. I had already started to watch a few programmes on the Makerston House television set, one of which seemed to be favoured by several of my fellow trainees. It was called *Rawhide*. Unfortunately, however, the actors spoke in very strong American accents.

I was very pleased when one evening Andrew suggested that we go to the Paisley cinema. I cannot remember the film we saw or, shall I say, tried to see because once inside, the cinema hall was so full of cigarette smoke that it made the screen look like it was suffering from a touch of condensation. Another new experience.

With Andrew's strict tutoring and my daily contact with people in the Head Office departments, my ability to communicate in English grew quite rapidly. I began to feel more confident within myself and even began to participate in the often lively, if not heated, discussions and debates amongst my fellow trainees during our shared dinner.

With such easy access to the house bar, albeit at our own expense, many of these discussions lasted well into the small hours. It soon became quite obvious that several of my fellow trainees did not depend entirely on their official trainee allowance, but could rely on their own additional private means. My fellow trainee from Brazil seemed to be particularly well funded as he quite often bought rounds of drinks for all of us.

It must have been the last week of our training programme in the Glasgow Head Office whilst listening to the departmental manager explaining to us the Company's trademark policy and brand protection that I suddenly felt a strong pain in my lower abdominal area. Andrew was told to take me straight back to Paisley and to call in at the Paisley Royal Infirmary for a check-up. Unfortunately, the train journey to Paisley led to the pain level increasing significantly. When finally we reached the hospital the doctors diagnosis was instant – appendicitis.

I remember Andrew speaking to the doctor at some length, obviously explaining my personal background and circumstances, but thereafter I only remember lying in a comfortable bed with a young nurse looking down at me with a big beaming smile. Underneath my shroud-like garment I noticed a large patch of plasters and bandages.

Shortly after becoming fully compos mentis again, a young doctor appeared beside the nurse and with a deliberately slow voice he explained to me that I had suffered from acute appendicitis and that I had had to be operated on without delay.

He assured me that the operation had gone very well and that after three days at the hospital I could return to Makerston House. However, I should rest there for at least a week. Once again, I felt that I was in good and competent hands and above all, the pain was gone.

The following morning had another surprise in store.

The previously empty bed opposite me was now filled with a new arrival. The nurse explained to me that it was a young boy from one of the islands on the west coast of Scotland and she thought it was the island of Barra. Apparently he had suffered serious injuries on one of the fishing boats and had to be airlifted from the boat by helicopter to be flown directly to Paisley and had undergone a lengthy emergency operation during the night.

"You will soon see another nurse appearing," she said, "and you will hear them conversing in a language, which I myself do not speak or understand."

And so it was. The sound of Gaelic, which must have been the only language this young boy could speak, had no resemblance to the English I had learnt so far or even to the colloquialisms used by large sections of the wider public in Glasgow and in Paisley.

I remembered that back home in Germany I had struggled at times to cope with the strong idiomatic differences between northern and southern regions of the country, including our Swiss neighbours, but in the end it was still the same structure and grammar. Now I could not make out a single word of what the nurse and the patient were saying to each other, but I must admit there was a pleasant and melodic sound to it. I now had something else to add to my list of discoveries in this exciting but strange land.

Later on, my nurse, whose name was Ann, informed me in more detail that the young boy had suffered life-threatening injuries when a steel rope used for hauling in the nets had snapped and had caused deep cuts along the whole left side of his body. Judging by the way his whole body was wrapped up in bandages I could well imagine the severity of his injuries. I felt quite touched when later during the morning, the young boy raised his hand slightly and waved across to me with a smile on his face, to which I responded in a likewise manner. He looked a few years younger than myself and I really wished I could have spoken to him.

With Nurse Ann appearing at regular intervals to take my pulse and check my temperature, my first day at the hospital seemed to pass very quickly, on top of which I was virtually pain free.

It was early in the evening when another nurse suddenly arrived to put up a screen between myself and the young boy from Barra. Having done that she informed me that a group of young men were waiting to see me. And so it was. Andrew and half a dozen of my fellow Makerstonians had come to see me. Andrew jokingly said that coming to see me was merely an excuse and that the main purpose was to utilise my presence here to have a look at the nurses as potential candidates to be invited to weekend parties at Makerston House. In fact, he said the prospects look already very promising because on entering the hospital a number of nurses suddenly appeared in the reception area, clearly intrigued by the arrival of such a large group of well-dressed young men.

"Judging by initial reactions," he said, "I am sure, we can count on a good number of acceptances when the day comes."

I said that I might possibly add another nurse to that list who is presently off-duty

On the fourth day, after a brief inspection by the doctor, I was informed that I could return to Makerston House and that an ambulance would take me there. All ran very smoothly and when dressing myself Nurse Ann even reminded me not to forget my precious bowler hat. The bilingual nurse also arrived which gave me the opportunity to express my best wishes to my fellow patient from Barra who, with a smile on his face, wished me farewell with a handshake. He really looked a young man after my own heart and I felt sorry I could not get to know him better.

Back at Makerston House our matron and her husband welcomed me back like a long-lost son and provided me with all available comfort. The one thing I particularly appreciated was a big armchair in the large sitting room, right in front of the television set. Whilst my fellow trainees were out at work I watched television programmesalmost non-stop and after my week of enforced rest I felt that my level of understanding had made considerable progress.

Andrew in fact suggested that I was now competent enough to continue my training programme without his assistance and that he had already informed the Company Personnel Department accordingly.

That sudden revelation surely must have come as a shock to you. Now it was swimming without a life jacket.

Strangely enough, I felt quite pleased with Andrew's announcement. Firstly, I had already felt for some time that being my mentor and guardian must have restricted

Andrew's own private life considerably and secondly it confirmed to me that the Company appeared satisfied with the progress I had made so far. On top of it all, I now felt that my mentor had become a true friend and confidant.

After my rest period, our training programmes sent Andrew and myself in different directions. I now found myself teamed up with Benji, my fellow trainee from Chile who had an excellent command of English, although with an accent which seemed to make him particularly alluring to female members of staff in the Company.

Our next destination were the large Ferguslie mills on the outskirts of Paisley where over two weeks we were introduced to the primary stages of turning bales of Egyptian cotton into cotton threads. It was certainly not a job where a bowler hat was part of the expected dress code.

In the early morning, we joined a stream of people – mainly young girls – heading towards the factory gates. As I listened to the chatter around me I began to wonder if Andrew's recent accolade about my linguistic achievements had not been a little premature. It may have applied to the more cosmopolitan environment of the Company's Head Office in Glasgow, but it clearly did not apply to the environment here at the Ferguslie factory gate.

As instructed, we reported to the general manager who, after a short description of the factory lay-out, called a young man to take us to the changing room and subsequently to introduce us to the supervisors in the various departments. Now our new dress code was a grey overall.

According to our training programme, both Benji and I

were expected to stay together for the whole period of our first 'work experience'. This suited me well because now, with both of us being foreigners, I felt more on an equal footing which was not the case under Andrew's mentorship.

Our week on the spinning floor was particularly challenging. The high-pitch noise of the spindles was almost deafening and made us wonder how the young female operators could cope with it week after week without any ear protectors.

As became obvious one day, the noise certainly did not dampen their sense of humour or their desire for a bit of frivolity. It was our last day on this spinning floor when Benji, minutes before the official closing time, had gone into the changing room for the customary shower. Unnoticed by the supervisor and indeed myself, one of the operator girls managed to sneak into the male changing room, snatch all of Benji's clothing and towel from his locker and deposited her booty outside the changing-room door on the factory floor. Normally, when the factory whistle sounded to announce the end of the working day, workers, both female and male, rushed off to ready themselves for their return home, but on this day the girls on our floor did not appear to be in a hurry. It had clearly been a pre-planned plot by all of them, because here they were, all gathering outside the male changing-room door, waiting to see how Benji would cope with his dilemma. The girls also cleverly delayed me from reaching the changing room. And then it happened. Benji, having also heard the factory whistle must have assumed that the operator girls would have left the floor by now as had always been their habit in the past. With dozens of eyes fixed on the door of the changing room, a dripping wet and naked Benji opened the door greeted by a salvo of giggles from the waiting crowd. I rushed over to retrieve Benji's clothing from the factory floor, inviting a round of boos from the girls.

Benji's popularity with the female workforce at the Ferguslie Mill was ensured for the rest of our training programme there and wherever we went we could count on instant recognition and a furtive smile.

On our last day, the general manager called us into his office to give us a summary of how the various floor supervisors had assessed our work and the only reference to the shower room incident was a dry comment that as result of our presence some safety devices may have to be installed on changing-room doors.

No doubt, your experiences at the Ferguslie Mill became the subject of jovial banter at Makerston House.

It did indeed. In fact, Benji provided us with a string of revelations in the weeks to come which kept us all on tenterhooks.

Benji was by nature a very cheerful and easy-going character and we were all very intrigued to learn more about his past. We all considered him to be a Chilean, but he now revealed that he was actually born in Spain. During the Spanish Civil War his father had sided with the Republicans and after their defeat the whole family fled to

Chile. However, according to some old Spanish tradition his parents had betrothed him as a very young boy to an equally young girl from another family of their own social circle. Benji admitted that his parents still expected him to honour this commitment which clearly put him under considerable stress. He showed us a photo of what looked like a three-to-four-year-old girl, but he said, "I have no idea what she looks like today, and in any case I want to make my own choice whom to marry, if ever."

However, he felt that his parents' honour was also at stake here and that in a gentlemanly fashion he should at least travel to Spain to officially end this unwanted liaison.

A week or so later, Benji booked a weekend return flight to Madrid and a new drama unfolded. After handing in his passport at Madrid Airport he was asked to wait whilst his passport was being passed to a senior officer. When this officer finally returned Benji was informed that he was under arrest. His Chilean passport showed his place of birth as Spain and the authorities consequently regarded him as a Spanish citizen. A quick search must have revealed that Benji had never done his national service which at that time was compulsory for all young Spanish males.

Accompanied by a guard, Benji was allowed to retrieve his suitcase in the baggage hall and was subsequently taken to an office in the airport building where he was allowed to telephone the Company's offices in Barcelona with a request for legal help. The Legal Department in Barcelona must have sprung into action immediately to consult with the Company Head Office in Glasgow.

Benji spent a night in the airport detention centre but the following morning he was already informed that arrangements were being made for him to return to London on the next available flight. As became known later, the Spanish authorities had demanded a considerable fine which the Company had agreed to accept. We never found out how much was paid for Benji's freedom, except that someone in the Glasgow Head Office let slip later on that it was a king's ransom.

Soon after his return to Scotland, Benji finally wrote a letter to his parents and to the family of his unwanted fiancée informing them of the termination of this betrothal. All this had also made it abundantly clear that Benji would not qualify for any future management job in the Company's large operation in Spain.

I have to admit I am truly impressed by the caring and almost paternalistic attitude displayed by your Scottish employer.

Yes, Joseph, it was, as I myself would find out later, very much a feature of this Company.

Chapter 3

My training programme now took me to the large Anchor Mill right in the centre of Paisley. This time I was on my own. Having had the company of Andrew and more recently Benji to and from our place of work, it felt quite strange now setting off from Makerston House in the morning on my own.

Unlike Ferguslie, the Anchor Mill was a sprawling complex of large high-rise brick buildings. Again, at the entrance gate I joined a queue of workers and it struck me immediately that there were significantly more young male workers than I had previously noticed at the Ferguslie Mill.

The gateman pointed me in the direction of the General Manager's office where again I was received with a hearty welcome and the revelation that I was now the fifth trainee this year to be let into the secrets of thread making. I refrained from disclosing that during my apprenticeship in the Company's German subsidiary I had already gained some knowledge of the diverse processes which eventually led to a sewing thread on a wooden bobbin, but then the general manager probably assumed that like many of my fellow Makerstonians I had joined the Company soon after completing a university education.

The activities at Anchor Mill were much more diverse than those at Ferguslie Mill. It soon became clear that the heavy work in the dye house for instance required an all-male workforce. The contents in the huge dye vats bubbled like mini volcanos and standing near them exposed the workers to extreme heat. On my second day there the supervisor, warning me not to approach the vats too closely, told me that just before Christmas the previous year a young operator had fallen into a vat with fatal consequences.

Although I could claim some prior knowledge of the processes of thread production, I have to admit that the next few weeks made me realise that my apprenticeship in Freiburg had only taught me the very basics. I was fascinated by the work in the Technical Development Department, where young men were working on a variety of pieces of machinery or bent over large drawing tables with intricate-looking designs on large sheets of paper. I was told that with nylon and polyester playing an increasingly important part in the production of threads, many of the old traditional production processes had to be modified.

When I introduced myself to the supervisor in the Engineering and Maintenance Department I received a particularly warm welcome. He showed a strong interest in wanting to know about the present conditions at the Mez AG in Freiburg. The reason for this soon became clear. In 1947 the Company had sent him to Freiburg to help with the reconstruction of the Freiburg factory which had suffered severe damages during a bombing raid in November 1944. Strangely enough, people in Freiburg rarely spoke about the war by the time I arrived there in 1950 and also during my apprenticeship at the Mez AG, none of this was ever mentioned. I was therefore very interested to hear at Anchor Mill more about the past history of my employer in Freiburg. Whilst I had assumed that the Scottish ownership of the Mez AG was a post-war event, it now emerged that the liaison stretched back to the early 1930s. I also learnt that during the war, the Mez AG was a significant supplier of weaving yarns for the production of parachutes, thus turning it into a potential military target. The reconstruction was completed in 1948. The supervisor was surprised that I knew so little of the Company's history and expressed his desire to visit Freiburg again, for he had fond memories.

"Over there," he concluded by pointing at a large cupboard in the room, "is still a box full of drawings from my days in Freiburg when we rebuilt the factory."

That late afternoon, when I walked back to Makerston House I asked myself why I had to come to Scotland to learn about these happenings in Freiburg. Why had my close school friends or fellow members of the European Youth Movement never mentioned any of this? Or was it all due to the widely circulating mocking euphemism in both Germany and abroad, 'Don't mention the war'. Anyway, I felt very pleased with what I had learnt today

In the evening over dinner, my newly gained information added another interesting topic to the generally lively review of our training experiences during the day. Often these dinner table exchanges were packed with very personal assessments, not only of our 'Trainers' but also of the variety of younger female staff encountered during the day. Contributions from Benji were always received with special interest. My training programme at Anchor Mill continued for another two weeks and I had to admit that my earlier apprenticeship in Freiburg was a mere 'taster' of what thread making was all about, compared with the level of detail I was now asked to absorb.

At the end of my last week at Anchor Mill I received instructions to return to the Ferguslie Mill and to report to the Scottish Distribution Centre which was located in the grounds of the Mill.

Chapter 4

I was now introduced to the Sales and Marketing Organisation of J. & P. Coats Ltd which traded under the name of The Central Agency, or TCA in short. All of a sudden I saw myself confronted not only with the familiar reels and bobbins of sewing threads and boxes of embroidery yarns, but also rows of shelves with zip fasteners and a sizeable section with crochet and knitting needles plus a vast assortment of sewing needles. I now discovered that the stock control system I had used when in charge of the warehouse in Munich was exactly the same here in Paisley and was presumably applied to Company warehouses worldwide.

Whilst there was plenty of activity throughout the day, this training week lacked the stimulus I had felt during my time in the factories and Head Office departments and I was very happy when I was told that as from the next Monday I would be out on the road to accompany one of the salesmen for the Glasgow region. I was handed a boxful of business cards which identified me as an official representative of 'The Central Agency' and to complete my new status I also received a smart-looking leather case filled with samples, brochures and customer order forms. To my great relief, I was told that I could leave this weighty case at Makerston House for the following week as my mentor will be one of the sales representatives for the Glasgow region, fully equipped with the Company's sales and marketing kit.

This was now really going to be your first exposure to your host country, outside the safe environment of Company employees and your fellow trainees.

Safe is probably too strong a word, but you are right, Joseph, it went through my mind that from now on I would meet up with people who were not part of our Company family and therefore less accommodating and friendly than what I had experienced so far.

On my return to Makerston House I was informed that a Mr Stevenson had phoned to let me know that for our first day together he would pick me up from Makerston House. I was very pleased to learn that this gentleman was going to be my mentor because I had met him already when he visited the Ferguslie-based Scottish distribution centre and from merely exchanging a few words with him I gained a very favourable impression of him.

As it turned out, my week with him was a truly stimulating experience. All the firms we visited received us with warmth and friendliness which I thought reflected not only on my mentor's good relationships with his customers, but demonstrated also the general respect in which the Company was held. It was only on a few occasions that customers put some probing questions to me about my background. My years behind the Iron Curtain often aroused more interest than what I had done during the preceding war years. It almost felt as if the constantly rising tension over a new, potentially apocalyptic conflict between East and West had numbed the memory of a horrific confrontation which had ended only a few years earlier.

I was very impressed with the generous and often very artistic display of the Coats products and merchandising aids, not only in ordinary drapery shops but also in the textile sections of large department stores. The dominance of the Company products was clearly evident whichever establishment we visited. But then, the competition was also far away in France or my own homeland Germany.

I thought to myself that Mr Stevenson had quite a 'cushy' job compared with the competitive conditions his far-away fellow sales representatives in Germany had to cope with.

I thoroughly enjoyed my first week on the road, which was just as well as the next phase of my programme required me to travel on my own and on public transport to visit customers in a number of villages and hamlets in the Scottish Lowlands. When studying the map in preparation for my forthcoming task, I began to wonder if these often remote locations were specially chosen to test the stamina and endurance of future managers or whether it was a gesture, letting us see the beauty and diversity of the Scottish countryside. It occurred to me – and a few of my fellow trainees had the same opinion – that in addition to testing our stamina and versatility, the whole programme was constructed in such a way as to maintain contact and render a service to those smaller draperyand village shops, which the official regional TCA sales representative could only visit infrequently. Equipped with a list of strange-sounding places and names of existing customers, I set off on another journey into the unknown.

To my surprise, the first phase of my programme was a very enjoyable train journey right down to the Scottish/English border at Gretna Green. This was my one and only train journey for the rest of my solo travelling programme as a trainee salesman. From Gretna Green onwards I had to rely on bus services.

My very first call was at a small drapery shop in Gretna Green. Upon producing my TCA visiting card the lady owner took a rather prolonged look at my name on the card. She then looked up and said, "Are you Polish?" When I told her that I was German, she proceeded to tell me at some length that the only German she had ever met before was a POW who had worked on her sister's farm and who had been a very versatile handyman. In fact, her sister had been very sad when her POW helper was released back to his home country. When the good lady then insisted on wanting to know how and why I had come to Scotland I thought to myself that if this is going to be the general pattern at each visit I shall never achieve the suggested quota of visits and my sales figures will remain poor.

After a few more personal questions and a cup of tea and biscuits, the lady suddenly pulled a large sheet of paper out of a drawer with all her needs for threads, zip fasteners and needles neatly itemised.

"Since I have not seen your official TCA representative for quite some time," she said, "I can at least give you a worthwhile order."

I had to admit to her that this was a one-off visit and on leaving her shop she wished me all the very best for my future career. When I told her that I would now try to find an inexpensive inn or hotel for the night she pointed at two places just down the road which she said were very reasonably priced and which were popular with young people who for one reason or another had come to Gretna Green to be married at the famous Blacksmith Shop.

I do not think that I could have had a better start to my training in salesmanship than I had had on my very first call.

After a good night's rest, I shared my breakfast table with a young couple from Somerset in England who quite excitedly let it be known that they had a booking at the Blacksmith Shop for the following morning.

Were you not curious to find out why they had come from far away Somerset to be married at Gretna Green?

I was indeed curious but did not muster the courage to ask them. I gathered, however, from some of their hushed conversations that religious differences between their two families may have been one of the reasons for their presence here in Gretna Green.

The list of villages I had to visit during the next few days presented not only a challenge in pronouncing their names correctly, but also tested my ability to find direct or indirect bus connections. It reminded me of the days when as a youngster I had to find country bus routes to get into the border zone along the Iron Curtain.

My next stop was in a village called Ecclefechan. The customer was a general village store catering for the majority of needs of the local population. The owners were a very jovial-looking couple and having seen my TCA visiting card they asked me to make myself comfortable in their back-room office until they had dealt with a few customers. When casting my eyes round the office I noticed a photograph on the desk showing a young man in a grey-blue uniform. I instantly thought that this will be the couple's son and that he may not have come back from the last war. Would they, after having discovered that I was German, ask me to leave the premises immediately?

When they finally entered the office, and having apologised for letting me wait, their questioning was very similar to what I had experienced the day before in Gretna Green, with the exception that their son had been a POW in Germany and had spent two years in a camp in Bavaria. They proudly added that their son was now a manager of a large hotel in Edinburgh.

You must have felt relieved to have been spared a potentially painful situation.

There was always that lingering unease that one day I might encounter situations where people had endured hardship and the loss of family members during the war and that consequently they might bear a lasting and deep-seated grudge against anything German. But thankfully throughout my travelling days in Scotland, such a situation never arose. And yet, there was hardly a village in which I did not encounter a war memorial which testified to the sacrifices made by young Scotsmen, not only during World War One and World War Two, but also in many other conflicts throughout the world. It seemed to me that people here were able to face tragedies and hardship with an admirable amount of stoicism and did not indulge themselves overly in self-pity or anger.

Having secured another sizeable order in Ecclefechan, my next destination was the small village of Lochmaben, to the west of Lockerbie (which as you may recall, many years later in 1988 was the scene of a terrorist air disaster with worldwide reverberations).

The Lochmaben haberdashery shop was run by a softly spoken middle-aged lady who greeted me with a great sigh of relief.

"I began to wonder," she said, "if the TCA had forgotten me altogether."

Before I could even utter my excuses for such neglect a young girl appeared with a tray full enough to hold an afternoon tea party. Unless customers entered the shop now to require the lady's attention, I knew that this would become another drawn-out visit with lots of questions. And so it was.

Having answered a myriad of question about myself, I was given a full account of her own background, how she liked German composers like Brahms and Mendelssohn, whilst encouraging me to sample the scones and making sure my teacup was never empty. It was very clear that this lady looked upon my visit as a rare and welcome opportunity to hear about the outside world and she was going to make the most of it. Suddenly the young girl reappeared with a piece of paper and, after a quick perusal by the shopowner, it was handed to me. Another sizeable order for Coats products. Finally, as several customers entered the shop, I thanked her for her hospitality and the order and as a parting shot I told her that I would personally inform the regional TCA agent to visit her more regularly in future as the home-baked scones alone warranted a visit.

On my way north, back to Makerston House, my programme called for two more visits in Abington and finally Lesmahagow, where again I was received with friendliness and unsuppressed curiosity about my background. On top of this, sizeable orders for Coats products greatly helped my self-esteem and assured me that I could build up a good rapport with people outside the protective environment of the Coats Company.

After this first sojourn into the Scottish Lowlands I was quite looking forward to returning to the comforts of my own room at Makerston House and to enjoy the company of my fellow trainees.

Weekend parties at Makerston had already in the past achieved a certain level of notoriety. When several of my fellow trainees visited me during my brief stay at the Paisley Hospital, their banter with the nurses must have been very successful because they always responded enthusiastically to our invitations. For tomorrow, I was told, we were going to have a full house and Nurse Anne who had so caringly looked after me had indicated she had managed to change her shift to come as well.

After a week of hopping on country buses, seeking out places to stay for the night and constantly being exposed to questions about myself, Makerston House had become a most welcome refuge and now coming back to a house party felt like a reward for a challenging week,

A private residence, just across the road from Makerston House was owned by the Lochhead family. The lady of the house was a native of Cologne and having heard that a trainee from Germany was amongst the residents in Makerston House, I had some weeks earlier received an invitation to meet the family, including their daughter Sylvia. The ramifications of this social encounter, as it turned out, had a life-changing impact on my own future.

Whilst my fellow trainees were busy setting up the big hall for the party and arguing about the records to be played, I went across to the Lochhead residence to see if their daughter would like to attend tomorrow's party. With pleasure, she responded, but could she also bring her best friend Elaine along? Of course! I was already cherishing the moment when on my return to Makerston House I could tell my colleagues I had managed a double score.

And this is how this young girl Elaine entered my life, leading to a series of dramatic changes in the years to come

Sylvia quickly mingled with my fellow trainees and the invited guests, but Elaine was of a more reserved nature and clearly needed some encouragement to get into the spirit of the party. With Nurse Anne wasting no time in singling me out as her partner for the evening, this pretty-looking auburn-haired young lady drew the decided attention of my Spanish colleague who appeared to have the right approach to make her feel more relaxed in this rather noisy environment. It was only late in the evening, when both Sylvia and Elaine were beginning to indicate that they were expected back home at a respectable hour, that I really came face to face with Elaine and I quickly realised that behind this mask of shyness was a probing mind and quite a self-assured young person. When I explained to her that I came from Germany and that my adopted home town was Freiburg in the Black Forest she broke into a lively description of holidays she had spent with her mother in Switzerland and Austria.

We were just beginning to enjoy the flow of our discussion, when she looked at her watch and declared that she had to leave immediately, otherwise there would be trouble at home. A clear message that the domestic scene was strict and that parental instructions were ignored at one's peril. I really felt sad that our encounter had to be cut short so abruptly since I definitely felt the desire to learn more about this young woman.

On our way to the front door I explained to Sylvia and Elaine that my training programme for the following week would require me to visit a number of Coats customers in villages north of Glasgow, but that after my return I would quite like to meet up again.

"Why not come across to my home again when you are back and we can all have dinner together," said Sylvia. "I am sure my mother would love to have another chat with you in her own mother tongue and maybe Elaine can even bring her mother along if she is not busy with her insurance business. When you are back from the north we can fix a date and time."

I have to admit, Joseph, I was quite surprised how my initial suggestion for merely another meeting had so swiftly turned into what could possibly become quite a formal encounter

"Sounds perfect to me," I said, obviously showing a sign of astonishment on my face. If that was the case, it was certainly made worse when at this moment I suddenly felt a hand on my shoulder. Nurse Anne was standing right behind me, beckoning me to rejoin the party. Had she overheard some of the exchanges between Sylvia and myself? If so, she never mentioned it.

Nurse Anne certainly made the most of this evening and she and a colleague nurse were the last to leave the party. The hospital and the nurses' residence were only a short distance from Makerston House and both Andrew and I decided to accompany our two guests back to their quarters.

On our way back I remember Andrew saying, "Watch out, Wolfgang, Nurse Anne has cast her eyes on you, and she will not be shy in coming forward."

"You are absolutely right, Andrew," I replied, because on our walk back to the hospital Nurse Anne had already whispered to me that she would like to go to the cinema with me the following week.

Suddenly my upcoming week away in the Highlands,

selling Coats products again to softly spoken middle-aged ladies, however inquisitive they may turn out, looked like a very welcome escape to reduce my adrenalin level again after this eventful house party.

I have a strange feeling that suddenly romance might be in the air. I have been wondering for some time now why you have paid so little attention to the opposite sex. Surely with all your past travelling and, if I remember correctly, your very active social life in Munich, a few young beauties must have crossed your path.

I am not surprised by your question, Joseph. As a young apprentice at the MEZ AG in Freiburg I once had a kind of juvenile crush on a very attractive fellow apprentice, but all my efforts to attract her attention fell on stony ground. I never found out why I was completely rejected, but my friend Gert suggested that my origin from the eastern part of the country may have had something to do with it. The young lady in question came from a long-established Freiburg family and her parents may well have set their eyes on an eventual suitor from another local family. Whatever the reason may have been, it somehow dulled my interest in female company in the subsequent years. And with politics, sport and the business world being my main areas of interest I certainly found my male friends more responsive to these topics and activities compared with the indifferent attitude often displayed by female acquaintances. I found it quite difficult at times to show the expected enthusiasm when confronted by the often delicate and more emotion-driven behaviour of some female acquaintances. It is early days yet, but as you will find out later, my hitherto slightly dormant appreciation of the female world will certainly experience an awakening here in this foreign land, where from the outset the girls had a straight head start over me. They could all speak English fluently.

A fresh week of travelling now lay ahead of me. Andrew had already shown me photos and postcards of the rugged Highlands and pretty-looking villages nestling at the foot of mountains or alongside rivers and lakes (or lochs, in the local idiom). I was very much looking forward to this new adventure.

When I reported to the Ferguslie Distribution Centre to receive details of my week's travel programme, and also to refurbish my sample case with Coats products, good fortune was once again on my side. My earlier mentor, Mr Stevenson, had also come to the Ferguslie office to collect goods for a personal delivery to one of his customers. When I showed him my new travel programme he immediately offered to give me a lift in his car to the northern outskirts of Glasgow where I would readily find a bus connection to Callander, which was my first port of call for the week. Needless to say, I was delighted by this kind offer. During our journey he wanted to know all about my experiences during my previous week's travelling in the Lowlands.

"Up here in the north," he said, "people are a bit more reserved, but they are nosey just the same and you will not escape from having to endure a lot of questioning about yourself and your past."

The first stage of my journey took me to the historic city of Stirling, and from there it was only a short bus ride to Callander. A big poster at the bus stop left me in no doubt that this was a popular tourist centre with a history reaching back to Roman times. Overnight accommodation seemed to be in plentiful supply. I immediately liked the feel of this place and I was looking forward to two interesting days in this attractive location.

The long Main Street was an interesting mix of low-level domestic stone buildings interspersed with a large variety of shops and the occasional café. It all exuded an image of a self-assured and prosperous community. On my way down the street, looking for the name of my first customer, I stopped at a newsagent's shop to purchase a postcard, to let my parents see the kind of interesting places I was visiting.

A new surprise was waiting for me. A young man rushed into the shop and asked for three Woodbines. I first thought that he meant three packets of these cigarettes but no, he only wanted to buy three cigarettes. I thought to myself that this must be a true example of the proverbial Scottish frugality. If ever this young man travelled to the Continent he certainly would not find a tobacconist to sell him individual cigarettes.

My first call was a very impressive haberdashery shop with a lavish display of beautifully embroidered tablecloths. And the shopowner was once again a middle-aged lady, who added to the general ambience of the shop by wearing a richly embroidered blouse with patterns which seemed to have some resemblance to designs I had seen both in Munich and also in the Black Forest region. After introducing myself and having dealt with the initial formalities I complimented her on her attractive displays and also her almost continental-looking blouse.

"Yes," she said, "I have just come back from a holiday in Austria and could not resist buying myself this blouse."

When she added that she had visited Salzburg and had even picked up a few sentences in German, I felt sure that with such instant rapport I would eventually leave these premises with a sizeable order for Coats products. And so it was. Not only did I receive a substantial order, but since lunchtime was approaching and shops were closing down for a short break, the lady suggested that I leave my bags in her shop and take a stroll along the river which was a special feature of this town.

On my way to the river, I passed several display panels with posters encouraging the public to visit a multitude of nearby beauty spots. Callander really seemed to be like a gateway to the picturesque Highlands.

When I returned to the shop to pick up my bags, I told the shopowner that I would quite like to seek overnight accommodation here in Callander before travelling further north.

"A friend of mine runs a very comfortable guesthouse," she said. "It is just two hundred yards from here on the other side of this street. I will give her a ring to see if she has a vacancy."

Considering that I came here as a complete stranger, I was quite taken aback by the friendliness and freely extended helpfulness which I now experienced on this, my first visit to the Highlands. Had I not been told only a day before that folks in the Highlands are more reserved?

On my way to my next customer I passed the guesthouse, deposited my overnight bag and proceeded to my next commercial encounter.

Also located in the Main Street, this was quite different from the stylish establishment of my first call. It was a typical general store catering for all sorts of domestic needs, including gardening tools, seeds and kitchen utensils. One corner, however, was completely set aside for Coats products and a particularly large section for zip fasteners and crochet needles. After looking at some length at my visiting card, the storekeeper waved to a young boy and told him to check the display racks with me and to make out a list of items freshly needed and then to let him see it before placing the order. Unlike on most of my previous calls, there were no questions about who I was or if I was the new TCA representative taking over from the gentleman who had visited them in the past. It was all very perfunctory and almost impersonal and the call must have rated amongst the shortest during my short selling career.

As I left the shop I thought to myself that however much I may at times have disliked the excessive questioning by lady customers, it was together with cups of tea and the odd scone, a more pleasurable experience than this purely business-driven visit I had just completed. Then it also struck me that this was my first call to a male-only customer. I have to admit, Joseph, that all of a sudden I was wishing that my visits for the rest of the week would be to drapery and haberdashery shops with lady owners or managers in spite of the questioning I would have to endure.

Thankfully my silent wish was granted for all the visits for the rest of the week. By now I could almost anticipate the kind of questions my lady customers were going to raise and my responses had improved not only grammatically but also with a growing vocabulary.

My stay in Callander ended with another visit to a nearby village where a charming elderly lady was in charge of a shop specialising in hand-knitting wools. The variety of yarns and colours presented a picture to behold. After quizzing me about my own background I was given a vivid description of the origin of all these products, the different breeds of Highland sheep and the characteristics of their wool, how many of the colours are derived from natural vegetation in the Highlands – even tree bark and seaweed – and how many of the yarns are still spun by women in the surrounding hamlets. One could tell from the expression on her face that she took great pride in letting a stranger like me become aware of some of the old traditions in the Highlands, still upheld to this very day. I was truly fascinated by her story which probably would have continued for some more time, if it had not been for a customer entering the store and requiring the attention of the shopowner. With that she passed me a piece of paper.

"As you can see," she said, "I cannot give you an order for your famous embroidery threads, but I am a very old customer of your Company for your knitting needles, zip fasteners and sewing threads."

On my way back to Callander I pondered over what I had just heard. I saw myself back at the huge dye house at Anchor Mill with its enormous vats and the large drums of industrially manufactured dyes. Two different worlds.

There was to be another addition to this afternoon's experience. As the bus trundled along the road back to Callander, I suddenly noticed a herd of very strange-looking beasts in a field.

My staring at these animals prompted a fellow traveller next to me to tell me that these were long-horned Highland cattle. I had to admit that with their long furry coats and amazingly long horns, these creatures looked quite forbidding compared with the gentle black and white Friesians I got to know so well when I spent my wartime evacuation on the Marlow family farm in Mecklenburg, or which I had seen elsewhere on my travels on the Continent.

Back in Callander I consulted a map to plan the rest of my week's travelling. I realised that I still had some distances to cover, stretching from a small place called Killin to Aberfeldy and then onwards to what seemed to be a larger town by the name of Crieff. What other new surprises will this country hold in store for me?

The customer in Killin turned out to be a small local post office which serviced this small community with a variety of goods, including our Coats products. It was a very busy shop with the gentleman owner clearly being the postmaster and his wife attending to the retail side of this establishment. There was no time for long questioning about my background, and in a most apologetic manner I was asked to wait in a corner of the shop until the postmaster's wife had a chance to let me know their requirements. It was obvious that most of the shoppers knew each other and regarded this visit to the shop as a welcome opportunity to exchange their latest news. The intonation and accents were quite different from what I had experienced in the Lowlands the week before and from the decided whispering between some of the ladies I could only assume that their news was not for general consumption.

With another order in my bag, I eventually got a bus to Aberfeldy. Fog was rising from the river valley and with daylight now fading so much earlier I could only catch a few glimpses of a magnificent river running along the bus route.

It was nearly dark by the time I reached Aberfeldy, but in the well-lit town centre I had no trouble in quickly finding a poster advertising the location of nearby guest houses, hotels and restaurants. To my surprise this town also seemed to have a railway station.

After the by now familiar signing in procedure I felt ready for a good night's rest, wondering what the following day would bring. According to my programme, I was to visit two customers in this town.

The arrival of autumn was no longer deniable. There was a decided chill in the air as I stepped outside in search of my first customer. Although the hills seemed quite a distance away, I could see a white dusting on their peaks.

My first call to an attractively decorated shop in the main town square provided a package of surprises of an unusual nature. After a relatively short probing into my own background and after having dealt with the business aspect of my visit, the lady owner was very anxious to tell me more about the history of her home town.

"Were you aware," she said, "that the Romans had come up north right up to Aberfeldy?"

I told her that I was not very familiar with Britain and her Roman past and I had always assumed that Hadrian's Wall was where Roman Britannia ended.

"In fact," I said to her, "I was already astonished when I was made aware of Roman ruins in Callander."

"Well," she said, "Callander may have old ruins, but Aberfeldy has a much more exciting story to tell. The famous – or shall I say infamous – Pontius Pilate was born here."

I found it quite difficult to hide my expression of disbelief. Pontius Pilate from Aberfeldy? That was stretching it a bit. My early mentor Andrew had once mentioned to me the mystery of the Loch Ness monster and I thought to myself that the Pontius Pilate tale falls most likely into the same category.

I thanked her for her interesting history lesson, although when I bade her farewell and thanked her for her order for my Coats products, she said, "I can see it in your face that you do not believe a Scot was at one time a governor of Judea."

Well, I remember from my own history lessons that over the centuries Scottish people have settled in many parts of the world, but I did not realise that they also reached the pinnacles of power in the Roman

Empire. Your customers do provide some interesting eye openers.

The whole journey, Joseph, is a journey of discovery and I have to admit that I began to feel increasingly comfortable in this rugged but hospitable land on the northern fringes of my host country.

On my search for my next customer, I found myself on the banks of the River Tay and a short distance up river an imposing stone bridge was spanning the water. I had seen a few of these typically Scottish-looking bridges before but this one with its five arches was a truly magnificent landmark.

My next call did not provide me with a history lesson, but with a most delicious afternoon tea and Scottish shortbread, for which I have retained an affection to this very day. After concluding the business side of my visit, I had to bid a rather hasty farewell as I had to rush back to collect my overnight bag, pay the bill and catch the last bus to Crieff. The journey took me through undulating countryside but mountain ranges always visible in the distance.

Crieff turned out to be a much larger town than I had expected. At the bus terminal, numerous posters advertised the services of a range of guest houses and hotels, leaving the reader in no doubt that this was a major touristic centre.

The following morning, on my way to my first customer, I passed a very impressive-looking building which was the Crieff Railway Station. Since Crieff was my last port of call before returning to Paisley, it occurred to me that instead of the already pre-planned bus ride via Stirling, I might get a train back to Glasgow and Paisley. I decided to explore such a possibility but noticed from the timetable that the Crieff Railway line was only a feeder line to the main Scottish Highland railway system and that the last train of the day left far too early for me to make the three business calls which had been marked out for me on my travel programme.

My first call was once again a shop run by a middle-aged lady with a young female assistant who, as it turned out, was in fact her daughter-in-law. Hand-knitting wools were clearly the main theme in this shop, but the artistic display was elegantly rounded off with several trays filled with Anchor Tapisserie Wools and embroidery threads. It had all the makings for a good order, but then the young lady informed me that Mr McFarlane, the TCA representative for the region, had only visited them a fortnight ago and that they were now expecting to receive the ordered goods any day.

The young lady clearly felt a little bit sorry for me. She asked me to follow her to the rear of the shop where there was a display board with knitting needles, zip fasteners and a range of other accessories.

"Let us put at least one small order together for you," she said. "After all, you have come a long way from Germany. My husband was stationed for a while in your country after the war but then they shipped him out to Korea. He came back, but wounded in body and mind."

I felt very awkward at this moment and did not really know whether to express my condolences or to say nothing. Not knowing the right English words for such an occasion, I decided on the latter. The lady in any case sounded a strong woman who probably would not wish to be comforted by a stranger with formal sympathies which, by the nature of the circumstances, would sound rather shallow.

I thanked the two ladies for not letting me leave empty handed but it crossed my mind at this stage that my next two calls may also have been preceded by a visit from Mr McFarlane.

On my way to James Square it struck me that this was a prosperous community with well-clad people in the crowded main shopping street. The solid stone houses all looked well cared for and when I saw the first signpost to the Hydropathic Centre I realised that this was probably an additional attraction to lure people to this typical Highland market town.

My fear about Mr McFarlane was unwarranted. It was a small corner shop in the Square, probably too small to warrant his regular attention. The shopowner was a very young lady, who looked more like someone who had just left school. As it turned out she had just completed her studies at Glasgow University and her father had set her up in this small shop to market modern design tapestry, cushions, embroidered table mats and other household items. She certainly was a bubbly young lady who spoke so fast that I had problems following her. After having extracted my curriculum vitae from me, which I had by now perfected to such an extent that I could run through it in about eight minutes, she told me that she did not actually sell our products in her shop but that she needed them for a group of women who produced her sales items in their own homes.

"Not having seen a TCA representative for the last three months," she added, "I was about to telephone the Paisley Office to place an order with them. Your visit is indeed most timely."

I was promptly presented with a list of her requirements and with a group of customers entering the shop I had a perfect opportunity to bid my farewell and also to congratulate her on the artistic and modern designs in her shop. She certainly was the youngest customer I had come across so far, on top of which she was also a very attractive young lady.

My next call was only a short walk away in the main shopping street. On my way, I wondered if this customer had also had a recent visit from the official TCA representative. After all, this was now my last call on my sales training programme in Scotland and I would have liked to finish it all with a worthwhile order. It all felt a little like getting close to the finishing line after a long race.

When I reached the designated address, the shop window displayed an array of what seemed to be fine tableware, cups and saucers, plates and beautiful terrines and bowls. Only the richly embroidered tablecloth, providing a colourful background to the whole display, suggested that this might after all also be a customer who is interested in Coats products. I entered hesitatingly, wondering what to expect. The surprisingly small shop was clearly favoured by the wider public as it was filled with several ladies, queuing up to pay for their purchases at what looked like an antique silvery cash register which produced a loud bell-like sound every time a large tray came shooting out from the lower part of this machine.

The range of merchandise was quite astonishing, ranging from tableware to cutlery with elegantly shaped horn handles, tartan ties and cushions, Highland souvenirs, postcards and, to my relief, also a large cabinet with a wide range of Coats products.

The lady behind the impressive cash register had already given me a fleeting glance as I entered the shop. With two bags in my hands she must have guessed that I was probably a commercial traveller. When I presented my visiting card to her I almost expected her to say that Mr McFarlane had just been to see her, but to my relief she said, "How timely for you to have come, I have a long list of things I need, business has been very brisk these last few days. Once the days get shorter knitting and embroidering always seems to become a favoured pastime amongst my local customers."

After answering the expected questions about myself and explaining the background to my visit, I also confided in her that my visit was my very last call on my Scottish sales training programme.

"We shall have to make it a memorable order then," she said, "but we also have to be quick because I have a lunchtime appointment during the closing hour."

The shopowner's decisive and confident behaviour very much appealed to me and after having noted down a sizeable order for a range of Coats products I asked her if I could leave my two bags in her shop during the lunch break as my bus for Stirling was only leaving mid-afternoon and I wanted to have a closer look at this interesting town.

"Of course," she said, "Just leave your bags over there in the corner. I shall be back at two o clock."

As we left the shop I decidedly saw her locking the door and with a brief goodbye we both headed off in opposite directions.

On my earlier visits to villages in the Scottish Lowlands I had already noticed the presence of eye-catching war memorials, which recorded not only the names of the local men who had lost their lives but also the places where the armed conflict had taken place. In some cases, these war memorials acted visibly as a solemn reminder of Britain's past as an empire builder, with dates stretching way back beyond the First and Second World Wars.

Here in these Highland villages and towns these memorials seemed to be equally widespread. When approaching a major road junction here in Crieff, I once again faced an impressive-looking war memorial surrounded by a colourful display of autumn flowers and shrubs. The large number of names chiselled into the bronze plates were a visible reminder of how this town had suffered from being called upon to provide their husbands and sons for resolving conflicts in often far-flung parts of the globe. But then I had also heard that in many cases these hardy Highlanders did not need much encouragement to test their courage and endurance in all kinds of adversarial circumstances.

On my wanderings, I suddenly found myself back in James Square and I felt very much drawn to having another look at the shop where I had made my second visit this morning. It was not really the shop I necessarily wanted to see but I would have liked to have another glimpse of that attractive young shopowner. However, lunchtime closing hours were clearly widely observed in this town and the little cornershop looked deserted.

With the time for my final departure, approaching I decided to return to the shop to retrieve my two bags.

On approaching the shop, I saw the lady owner standing outside the entrance door talking to a helmeted policeman and a gentleman in civilian clothing.

The shopowner must have spotted me as she waved to me to come closer.

"There has been a break-in during lunch time," she said, "but they have thankfully only raided my cash till. Your two bags are still where you left them."

The gentleman in civilian clothing was clearly puzzled by this remark and wanted to know why I had deposited two bags on the shop premises. I produced my TCA visiting card and with supporting interventions from the shopowner, we explained the purpose of my visit and the reason why my bags had been left at the shop. However, the gentleman, who I had gathered by now was a plain cloth policeman or detective, decided to question this 'stranger' further. When did you leave the shop, where have you been during the last hour? I almost expected a body search or a command to follow him to the police station for further questioning, but thankfully nothing like this happened.

There was no broken window or signs of a forced entry into the shop and the access must have been achieved by unlocking the main door without arousing any suspicion to passing traffic.

I was allowed to collect my two bags and, after expressing my sympathy to the shopowner for this misfortune and a rather formal goodbye to the two policemen, I headed off to catch my bus to Stirling with my final destination – Makerston House in Paisley – increasing in appeal by the hour.

Did you ever find out if the perpetrator was eventually caught?

No, I did not but the whole episode provided nevertheless a welcome extra topic for the dinner table at Makerston House.

Covering the last stretch from Glasgow to Paisley by train, I felt quite elated, almost like coming home. As the taxi finally pulled up outside the main entrance to the house, Benji was the first one to greet me, beaming as ever.

"Come and join us in the bar," he said, "you look quite worn out."

"You have the whole weekend to recover," he added, "because the next house party is only in a fortnight's time and Anne and her friend will also be coming again. We have not contacted the half-German girl from across the road yet and we thought that with your personal contact to her family, you might do the asking."

That did indeed suit me very well, because the girl's invitation to make contact again after my return from my Highland tour had by no means been forgotten.

When I finally reached my room, I slumped myself into my comfortable armchair with a profound feeling of elation and also thankfulness. Is it possible that St John's Chapter 15, Verse 16 was more than just a random reference on my Confirmation Certificate?

My mind started wandering back to the turbulent events during my formative years, the often inexplicable escapes from misfortunes, the joys of true friendships and a caring family. And now here in a foreign land I had once again found shelter, acceptance and the prospect of new friendships and more. How long will this last? On the small dressing table I suddenly noticed a letter and a postcard which had arrived during my week's absence.

The address was in my father's distinctive handwriting. My mother had told me once before that my father was a very reluctant letter writer but strangely enough he always insisted on writing the addresses on the envelopes which, she told me, he regarded as his contribution to the family correspondence. He also made the disputable claim that my mother's handwriting was not good enough and that her scribbles would cause problems in the mail sorting offices. Receiving letters from one's family should be a joyous occasion, but at the same time they can also be the carriers of sad and unpleasant news. Into which category would this letter fall? I decided to leave the opening until later, but had a quick look at the postcard from Munich on which my old friend Walter reported in his much appreciated laconic style that the OktoberFest will be held again, even without my presence. He will drink an extra Stein to my health.

Late at night I finally opened the family letter to learn that after our paternal grandmother's death in 1955 our grandfather had now followed her to her resting place.

Before leaving Freiburg I had already noticed a growing decline in his mental and physical health after my grandmother's death and the news in the letter did not come as a complete surprise. Otherwise the family appeared to be in good health and with Christmas approaching rapidly, my mother took the opportunity to raise a host of questions. How early can you come? How long will you stay? Will you come by air or rail? If by air, which airport will you be coming to?

Whilst these were quite reasonable questions, it struck me that my mother seemed decidedly less concerned with my travel details when as a young boy I did my journeys across the Iron Curtain.

I reckon, Wolfgang, that in those early days, desperate circumstances and the realisation of one's inability to influence events may well have led to a reduced display of natural maternal concerns. Your mother must have suffered terribly every time you set off on those journeys. Also remember that in your father's absence you, although still very young, were the senior male in the family and your mother may not have seen you only as her little boy. Now, living again in a secure environment, it no doubt gives her great pleasure to openly mother you again.

That sounds like a fair and succinct analysis, Joseph. Thank you.

Chapter 5

During my past week's travelling I had found myself thinking quite frequently about the invitation from Sylvia and Elaine to contact them again after my return from the north. Would I break local conventions if I gave Sylvia a ring on a Sunday? In any case, what could I say to her? Amongst the correspondence awaiting me in my room I had expected a letter with details of my training programme for the next week and beyond but there was none.

It was over breakfast when my mentor Andrew came up to me holding a letter in his hand.

"Very sorry," he said. "They gave it to me last Friday at the Personnel Department in Glasgow to pass on to you personally."

I was quite relieved to see that after a debriefing day at the Ferguslie Distribution Centre I was asked to visit the Glasgow Head Office again for familiarisation with several administrative departments. Thereafter, however, I was instructed to travel south to a town called Leicester to sell and promote the threads to industrial enterprises.

"They do not let us rest on our laurels," Andrew remarked when I told him about my forthcoming movements. His own training programme had so far concentrated mainly on the mills and Head Office departments and the challenges of selling and promoting Coats products still lay ahead of him. After having been my valued mentor from the day I arrived at Glasgow Central Station, I thought to myself that after only a few months I was now the one who could give him a few suggestions for the forthcoming part of his own training programme.

The highlight of the new week was an invitation by Sylvia to join her family for dinner at their house on Wednesday evening. Elaine and her mother would also be present. When I got the message, I was not sure whether I felt elated or if a slight feeling of fear had gripped me. Shall I, as before, bring a bunch of flowers just for Sylvia's mother or should I take something also for Elaine and her mother? When I asked Andrew as to what the local etiquette would require of me, his rather unhelpful reply was that he had never been in such a situation, but if he was me he would only take some flowers to the lady of the house. I decided to go with that piece of advice.

After a brief visit to the Ferguslie Distribution Centre I proceeded to my appointments in the Company's Glasgow Head Office, once again properly attired with my bowler hat which I enjoyed wearing more and more. It felt like a symbol of status apart from giving me an extra few centimetres in height.

As on previous visits I was received by all staff members with the utmost courtesy and friendliness and I was also given more details about my 'industrial' training in Leicester. Accommodation was already pre-booked for me and the local sales representative would provide me on arrival with a detailed work programme. I have to admit I was truly impressed by the almost paternal care and the organisational skills so generously extended to me. I could only assume that maybe management trainees were given this kind of support and guidance to instil in them the standards expected of them in their own future management roles.

Finally, Wednesday evening was upon me and, equipped with a bunch of flowers, I crossed the road from Makerston House to the residence of the Lochhead family. Sylvia opened the door with a cheerful, "Come on in! Everybody is here, but Elaine's mother and my father are huddled in the morning room probably discussing some insurance business. I am sure they will not be long because Elaine's mother has already expressed great interest in meeting you."

After disposing of my flowers to the lady of the house I finally came face to face with Elaine again. She looked even more attractive than what I remembered of her at the Makerston House party, and with my newly acquired knowledge of Highland places the flow of our conversation was easy and unconstrained. By gentle manoeuvring I quickly found out that Elaine was an only child and that her mother had been widowed when Elaine was only nine years old. Guessing Elaine's age at about 18 to 19 years I felt reasonably sure that her mother was not a war widow, although I knew only too well from my own wider family how the traumas of the war years led to several premature male deaths in the early post-war period.

Whilst these thoughts were quickly passing through my mind, Elaine's mother entered the dining room. Immediately one was left in no doubt, this lady oozed personality but

I thought she also had a warm and friendly countenance. Since she was clearly very friendly with Sylvia's German mother I came to the conclusion that my own German background would not be an obstacle to developing some closer relationship with her daughter.

Between Sylvia's mother engaging me in questions about present day life in West Germany and Elaine's mother probing unobtrusively into my family background, my exchanges with Elaine across the dinner table became somewhat sporadic. Yet there were promising eye contacts between us which made me feel that there could be a follow-up to this encounter. At a momentary lull in the table conversation I managed to let the party know that my next training programme would take me to Leicester and that after my return and possibly a few more days at the Glasgow Head Office I hoped to be given leave to return to Germany for Christmas and the new year.

As I was about to bid my farewell to the party, Elaine's mother took me aside and suggested that after my return from Leicester I might like to give them a call to arrange an evening get-together at her home in Elderlie. I really felt like having struck gold and thanked her, almost too enthusiastically, for her invitation.

Back in my room at Makerston House, my mind went over the events of the evening. Am I just being invited because I am a foreign curiosity? Surely attractive girls like Elaine and Sylvia will have local boyfriends? Am I chasing shadows?

At the door, my goodbye to Elaine culminated in

a deliberately prolonged handshake when I suddenly remembered that I was supposed to ask her and Sylvia to come again to another Makerston party the following Saturday. I added that I could not guarantee to be there myself but was hopeful that I could leave Leicester early enough that day to be back in time for the party.

The railway journey to Leicester was comfortable albeit longer than I had expected. After leaving Glasgow I enjoyed seeing again the undulating countryside with some higher peaks now showing a white dusting at their heads. It gave me an odd feeling to think that only a short while ago this had been my first testing ground to see how I would cope with the challenge of not only selling to customers in a foreign land but also with the logistics of finding my way around an unknown territory.

Considering what you told me before about your perilous travels as a young boy in Eastern Germany at least now you did not have to look back over your shoulder to avoid policemen or border guards.

Very true, Joseph. Comparing my early travels with the challenges here, this has, in the true meaning of the word, been a piece of cake. Instead of fear and suspicion I was now showered with a level of hospitality and friendliness which had exceeded all my expectations. Can I expect the same in Leicester? Was it one of those cities which had gone through the traumas of heavy bombing raids during the war and if so, will people have long memories?

Outside the railway station, taxis were coming and going

at short intervals and when I hailed one of them I was quite surprised to find a driver with what looked like Indian or Pakistani features. I showed him my piece of paper with the address of my prearranged accommodation and when he replied that he knew the area very well I noticed already the distinctly foreign twang in his voice. I was going to hear a lot more of it in the days to come.

My home for the next few days was a pretty-looking terraced house in Fosse Road. The owners were an elderly couple by the name of Chapman. From the moment Mr Chapman opened the door I knew that I had once again landed at the right place.

"Your Company has sent young men to us before," he said, "and we have always found them to be interesting company."

"Well," I replied, "I hope I can continue with that tradition."

After also meeting the lady of the house and having settled into my comfortable room, the local TCA sales representative telephoned to inform me that he would visit me the next morning to provide me with a list of the customers to be visited.

The evening meal with the Chapmans quickly revealed not only a very charming but also an extremely well-educated couple who displayed a knowledge and interest in a vast variety of topics including the historic complexities of Continental Europe. My earlier active involvement in the European Youth Movement found their particular interest and led to a discussion well into the late hours.

The following morning our official sales representative arrived with a detailed list of existing customers to be visited. When he saw me looking somewhat startled when reading the location Loughborough on the list he quickly assured me that it was merely a short bus ride away. During the general briefing session, I got the impression that the majority of these enterprises were producing merchandise for the well-known retail chain Marks & Spencer. What he failed to mention was that most of the managers and buyers I was going to meet were, like the taxi driver, of Asian descent.

The industrial world of Leicester and its surroundings quickly revealed itself as a tough training ground. It was a far cry from the welcoming and friendly atmosphere, the cups of tea and scones I had enjoyed so much on my travels in Scotland. Now it was a matter of having to wait in often uncomfortable waiting rooms until the manager or buyer was ready to see me, deal with requests for technical assistance, or to speed up orders already placed and not infrequently to receive a more than just gentle hint that the Coats prices were too high. Nobody seemed to have the time to ask me any personal questions, which in a way was quite a relief, but the relentless emphasis on speed, efficiency and commerce-related issues turned my days into a form of routine occupation. However, the values of my orders booked every day far exceeded those ever achieved on my travels in Scotland. I had to confess to myself that commercial success is after all the overriding priority and personal preferences and sensitivities had to be put aside.

The challenges during the day were fully compensated

for by the lively and stimulating discussions every evening with my landlord couple. It made me completely forgo exploring the city of Leicester or go to the cinema. I was fascinated by Mr Chapman's deep knowledge of British history, the Empire and its recent gradual unravelling and his own analytical assessment of why Germany fell so easily under the spell of a demagogue like Hitler.

"If Lloyd George had not been so vengeful at Versaille in 1919," he said one evening, "1939 might never have happened."

"After all," he added, "it was an armistice and not a capitulation or surrender."

It was strange to hear such words from an Englishman as they almost echoed views expressed by my own parents when as a young boy I confronted them in the aftermath of the war with questions as to how this tragedy could ever have happened.

I was glad to learn that all members of my landlord's wider family had survived the war years unscathed.

"Somehow," Mr Chapman added, "the Luftwaffe thankfully must have regarded Leicester as a target of lower strategic importance because after a severe air raid in November 1940 the city escaped further serious attacks."

By the time it came to Friday evening, there were not many details of my own past which Mr Chapman had not diligently extracted from me and which had become the opening to so many lively and memorable exchanges. My training week in Leicester had certainly tested my stamina but at the same time I shall always look back on it as my introduction into the fascinating and often turbulent history of my present host country.

When the taxi arrived on Saturday morning to take me to the station I felt quite emotional when bidding my farewell to this very hospitable and kind-hearted couple. We promised each other to maintain contact.

I presume that the imminent Makerston House party and your simmering interest in the girl from Elderslie made you chose the earliest train back up to Scotland?

I certainly did, Joseph, and even more surprisingly when filling the hours on the train with writing my report on my training week in Leicester, my mind kept wandering off, thinking of what I could or should do at the evening party to gain the full attention of this young girl. There will be Nurse Anne who will most likely repeat her wish to be taken to the cinema. And then there was also Elaine's mother's invitation to visit them one day at their home. All this was overshadowed by the question of when and for how long I would be allowed to return to Germany for the Christmas and new year break.

When I finally arrived at Makerston House my colleagues proudly informed me that all the female guests from the last party had agreed to join us again and that furthermore all trainees had received their letters about the arrangements for the festive season. My letter was pinned to the noticeboard.

To my delight I was informed that I was booked on a flight to Zurich on 22nd December with a return to Glasgow/

Renfrew Airport on 6th January.

Prior to my departure, I was to spend the remaining days in the Head Office department responsible for the Company's wide range of trademarks.

Preparations for the party were already in full swing and, after making myself presentable for the evening event, I joined a group of my colleagues who acted as the reception committee at the front door of the house. Nurse Anne and a few of her colleagues were the first to arrive, followed by a taxi with three ladies from a college in Glasgow who I learnt later had been invited by my fellow trainee from Brazil. He never revealed how he got to know these three ladies, but being a charmer by nature we were not surprised about his ability to attract the attention of the opposite sex wherever he went. As I had noticed with Benji before during our joint training period at the Ferguslie Mill, there was something about these young men from South America which seemed to stir the emotions of the female gender more easily than what we from more temperate climates could achieve.

My main concern at this moment however was where was Elaine and Sylvia? I was about to walk across the road to the Lochhead home when a torchlight appeared on the driveway and the two girls I had really been waiting for finally appeared.

With Nurse Anne having fallen under Benji's spell and Sylvia happily enjoying the attention of several of my fellow trainees, I now finally had a chance to gain Elaine's undivided attention, culminating in a couple of dances during which, to my embarrassment, I laid bare my clumsiness in coordinating my feet with the rhythm of the music. My lack of ever having attended dancing lessons in my younger days now showed up as a serious faux pas. Elaine on the other hand was a confident and clearly experienced dancer and only displayed a gentle frown when my feet got completely out of order.

Did you think that this now was the beginning of a serious relationship?

Yes, I think it was. A kind of sudden infatuation. Holding her close to me on the dance floor, smelling her perfume and listening to her soft Scottish voice, it all sent my head spinning. I would have loved to seal it all with a first kiss, but somehow the noisy and crowded party background did not seem the right moment to test the young lady's reaction to such an advance.

It was not long after this dance that one of my fellow trainees nudged me on the shoulder to tell me that a lady was waiting in the entrance hall ready to collect her daughter Elaine.

And that is how this memorable party ended for both of us. In the hall, mother and daughter had a short, hushed conversation which resulted in me being asked if I was free next Wednesday to come to their home for dinner, and if so Elaine would come to collect me in their family car. Needless to say, I was delighted to accept and promised that I would try my hardest to catch an earlier train back from Glasgow.

After they had both left in their Anglia car, I only rejoined the still-lively party for a short while and when Sylvia suggested that she ought to go home as well I escorted her back to her parent's home just across the road.

I was not quite sure if I should confide in her that I had been invited to Elaine's home, but realising that they were close friends who probably talked to each other every day, I decided to divulge my little secret to her

Sunday was a much-appreciated day for rest and recovery. The only pressing issue was to telephone my parents to let them know the details of my Christmas holiday. It was a Sunday, my mother quickly established, and clearly without any further consultation with my father she assured me that Papa would only be too pleased to drive to Zurich instead of his usual Sunday visit to Bad Krozingen where he sits for ages in the bubbling thermal waters. Her comments instantly stirred up old memories when the whole family used to pay visits to this thermal location where in those early days we used to sit in what looked like large drums and immerse ourselves in the warm waters with the open-air temperatures often below zero.

After lunch, I had a request from my Spanish fellow trainee which eventually led to some serious consequences for myself. Jose was a keen photographer and he had heard that prices for top-quality cameras were significantly lower in West Germany than they were both here in the UK or his homeland Spain. He knew exactly what he wanted and gave me a note with a precise description of the camera. I mentioned to him that some shops in Freiburg may be closed between Christmas and the new year but that I would do my best to locate a shop open for business.

He added that he would give me a down payment of £50 – with the full value to be settled after my return from Germany. He also suggested that I should leave my own camera at Makerston House and merely take the film roll with me for development in my hometown, since he assumed that my family would like to see the pictures I must have taken during my travels in Scotland. On re-entry into the UK I could then declare this new camera as my own personal property. Within the spirit of camaraderie that existed at Makerston House, I agreed to his proposal and together with the money, which he provided in English banknotes, I deposited everything in my wallet.

The days flew by very quickly. On Wednesday, shortly after my return to Makerston House, Elaine arrived in the buff-looking Anglia car. After a relatively short ride, which to my surprise took us past the familiar gates of the Ferguslie Mill and the Distribution Centre, we arrived in Elderslie at her home right at the top of a steep road.

In the darkness, the lights from the windows cast a warm glow over the garden and a turret on one side of the house gave it an almost castle like appearance. Elaine's mother, who after all I had only met once before, greeted me like a long-lost friend. From the moment I set foot in this house I felt very much at home. It had a warm and relaxed atmosphere and the glow from the fireplace added to the pleasant ambience of this residence. When even the young cuddly pet poodle Gay showed her approval by licking my outstretched hand it gave me an additional feeling of acceptance and I felt that this would probably not be my one and only visit to this house.

The conversation flowed easily about travelling experiences on the Continent and my own impressions of life in Britain and particularly Scotland. As to be expected, both mother and daughter were anxious to know much more as to how, all the way from the Black Forest in Southern Germany, I came to Makerston House in Paisley.

The evening was one of those rare events when one feels that something really important is happening. When I finally suggested that I should make my way back to Makerston House and enquired about public transport facilities, Elaine's mother offered to drive me back.

"It is rather late and the weather too inclement for young girls to drive around in cars," she said.

After exchanging best wishes for the coming festive days and thanking my hosts for a memorable evening, a short drive took me back to Makerston House. To crown it all, Elaine's mother suggested that after my return from Germany she would like to hold a party at her home to which I could also bring a few of my fellow trainees from other overseas countries. It struck me that holding parties must obviously be quite a popular pastime in Scotland.

Chapter 6

The last working day of the year finally arrived. With my suitcase fully packed with freshly cleaned clothing and a few souvenirs for my parents and brothers, on Sunday morning I finally set off from my adopted home by taxi to the Glasgow/Renfrew Airport. First stop London Heathrow, the size of which I found quite overwhelming. A uniformed young lady advised me to proceed to the adjacent terminal to fetch my flight to Zurich. It all looked and felt like a well-oiled organisation and when the passport officer finally, after another stamp in my passport, wished me a happy Christmas I thought to myself that I would not need much persuading to spend a lot more time in this country.

Zurich Airport looked quite small, almost provincial in comparison with what I had just left behind in London. My father was waiting at the arrivals gate. Whilst other fellow travellers were greeted by friends or relatives with shrieks and hearty embraces, I was merely received with a firm handshake.

You sound disappointed that you did not receive a more passionate reception from your own father.

No, far from it. In our family we have always been rather diffident in making a public display of feelings and emotions. This, I think does not only apply to my family but is a general hallmark of people from the northern parts of Germany. Strangely enough, this behaviour also seems to prevail amongst the inhabitants in my new host country Scotland.

Instead of choosing the windy route back through the Black Forest, my father decided to make the return journey to Freiburg via Basel.

"We have had heavy snowfall recently and some of the mountain roads could be quite perilous. In any case," he said, "the route via Basel will take us past Bad Krozingen again but your mother would not forgive me if we stopped for a quick dip in the thermal."

On our drive back I told my father about the request from my Spanish fellow trainee, whereupon he told me that he himself was a good customer at a leading Freiburg photographic shop and that they were open for business between Christmas and the new year. Furthermore, he said we might even get a discount on the full price. In any case, all shops would be open and busy tomorrow and he could make himself free in the afternoon to see if we could make this purchase.

In the privacy of our home, mother received me with a big hug, and my two brothers had to wait patiently before bombarding me with questions. It was a lovely feeling to be back home, but then I also had momentarily a strange sensation that this was not really a homecoming but that I had become more of a visitor.

The Christmas tree, laden with lametta, occupied the

usual corner in the sitting room. Over coffee and mother's home-baked stollen, which she said she had already baked in August, I was given a quick resume about life in Freiburg during my absence. I was virtually encouraged not to ask too many questions as they were more interested to hear how I had fared on the other side of the Channel.

"Lately you have followed in your father's footsteps by keeping written correspondence to an absolute minimum," my mother said, "so be prepared for a lot of questions." And there were plenty of them.

Was there a widespread anti-German feeling amongst the population? Were the damages from German air raids still visible? Had I encountered any personal insults? How was I treated in hospital for the removal of my appendix? What did I think of their cuisine? And when, after answering these questions I mentioned rather coyly that I had also met a girl to whom I felt very attracted, my parents exchanged glances which clearly displayed their high level of curiosity.

"Unfortunately, I cannot show you a picture of her yet," I said, "but I have the film with me which hopefully we can get developed during the next few days."

"I will drop it off at the photographic shop in the morning on my way to the office," my father quickly interjected, "and I am sure they will have it ready by the time we visit them in the afternoon for the purchase of the camera."

It was quite obvious that he was very anxious to see what this young lady from Scotland looked like.

It felt rather strange, sleeping in my own bed again, which I have to admit was not as comfortable as the one in my adopted new home Makerston House.

Freiburg presented itself in a very festive mood. Shop windows were abundantly decorated, the market around the Muenster was brimming with stalls of all descriptions, including the row of sausage stalls without which any self-respecting Christmas Market could obviously not exist. Even the bank had caught the Christmas spirit with a generously bearded Father Christmas standing at the door welcoming the customers.

When I presented my English banknotes for conversion into Deutsch Marks, the counter clerk insisted on seeing my passport and he also held each bank note up against a lamp before filling in a form with the amount due in Deutsch Marks.

I was pleased to receive 11 Deutsch Marks for each pound and I felt sure that Jose's down payment of £50 would go a long way to purchase the camera, hopefully later this afternoon.

On my way to meet my father, an employee from the MEZ AG suddenly nudged me on the shoulder, welcoming me back to Freiburg. When I explained to him that I was only here on holiday and that I would be returning to Scotland very shortly he was curious to hear more as to why I had been sent to that faraway place. I gathered from all this that the details of my secondment to Scotland were not common knowledge within the Company here in Freiburg. I declined his invitation to join him for a coffee with the genuine excuse that I was on my way to meet my father, which spared me from any further questioning by this young

MEZ employee.

The owner of the photographic shop greeted my father with handing him an envelope.

"Interesting pictures," he said. "We do not see many of those here in Freiburg."

They had indeed developed my film that very same morning as a special gesture to my father. When I produced Jose's piece of paper with the description of the camera, the shopowner just took a quick look and promptly confirmed that he had that precise model in stock.

"Your friend seems to know something about photography," he said, "as he has chosen a high-quality camera with a rather expensive Zeiss lens. I am afraid this camera will cost you slightly over DM700 but with Christmas just round the corner and your father being a longstanding customer, I can help you with a small discount of 15 percent. The development of the film you can regard as a gift from me."

I had already told my father that Jose's down payment of £50 had only given me DM 540 but that he would pay me the balance on my return to Scotland. My own financial resources were already dangerously low and when my father saw me fumbling around in my wallet to see if I could muster the total amount required, he quickly offered to help me out with the missing balance. Considering that in our younger days my brothers and I were always kept on very meagre pocket money allowances his current offer of support was much appreciated.

When the shopowner finally retrieved the camera from

the storeroom I saw immediately that this was a different class from my own simple Agfa camera left behind at Makerston House. The deal was done at a total cost of DM 612 and I put both the invoice and Jose's note safely away in my wallet.

On our way home, I asked my father if he had any idea as to why the clerk at the bank had gone through an extra checking process of the English notes I had handed over. There were rumours, he said, that towards the end of the war Germany flooded the international financial markets with high-quality forged English bank notes of which some still appear to be in circulation. My father was quite surprised when I told him that a number of Scottish banks were authorised to issue their own bank notes and that they, although looking very different, are full legal tender throughout the whole country. A strange system, my father replied adding that he would like to have a look at some of them on my next return visit.

Although there was no carp soup on Christmas Eve, the festive days followed the traditional pattern crowned by mother's delicious Christmas goose and my favourite Brussels sprouts, which to my astonishment had only rarely appeared in the culinary offerings in England or Scotland.

My photographs from my travels in Scotland and England aroused great interest and, as to be expected, two of them depicting Elaine received my parents' particular attention. My father even went so far as to describe her face as angelic, a word that presumably rolled off his tongue because it was Christmas.

The Christmas service in the Johannis Church was rather poorly attended, which our pastor attributed to the perilous road conditions caused by a sudden heavy snowfall. However, pavements were quickly cleared in the ensuing days with lashings of reddish-brown salt and I was able not only to meet up with my close friends Gert and Klaus but also to pay a visit to the Riesterer family who so generously had given us shelter when we first arrived in Freiburg in 1950.

You mentioned earlier on that on your return to your family you felt almost like a visitor. Did this feeling persist as the days went by?

Strangely enough, the feeling of a true homecoming grew stronger day by day. Sharing memories with one's friends again, walking old familiar paths, visiting cafés where the waitress still remembers you and reconnecting also with my uncle Erhart's family were all powerful emotional experiences which restored quite quickly my feeling of belonging. Yet I also did not seem to dread the day when the aeroplane would take me back to Scotland.

Freiburg greeted the arrival of the new year with a noisy display of fireworks and clearly visible against the night sky it was obvious that also the neighbouring villages did not want to be left out with their contribution to this annual spectacle.

The first week of the new year gave me a long overdue opportunity to attend a classical concert at the Freiburg City Theatre. I also went to the cinema to watch an American film about the war in the Pacific, where I was glad to have the help of German subtitles because although I thought that by now I had mastered the English language quite well, the American English still sounded like a different language to me.

Prior to the day of my departure my father informed me that due to a pressing obligation in his office I would have to return to Zurich by train, which I did not mind at all. I had become very fond of travelling by trains. After all trains had played such an important and memorable role in my life as far back as my boyhood days in the post-war years in Eastern Germany.

My suitcase was bursting with extra clothing because my mother insisted that with Scotland being so much further north than Freiburg, winters up there must be much harsher. I was also given an extra small case filled with a large stollen cake neatly wrapped in tinfoil, plus a small tin with her homemade marzipan balls. There was also room for the new camera and a side pocket for my wallet and travel documents.

As so many times before, my mother came with me to the station with the parting reminder that I should write more regularly again, which I promised to do.

After a change of trains in Basel, I reached Zurich Airport in good time for my departure to London and the scheduled onward connection to Glasgow. I booked in my suitcase but retained my new small case as cabin luggage. All ran very efficiently. I felt very relaxed and my mind began to refocus again on Makerston House, my fellow trainees and what tasks may lay ahead of me.

After a smooth passage through the London passport control and another stamp in my passport, which I treasured very much, I proceeded to the luggage hall to retrieve my suitcase.

Customs clearance of all luggage had to be done at London Airport before proceeding on internal flights to other destinations in the United Kingdom. As I was about to walk past two uniformed officers, one of them stepped forward and asked me where I had come from and if I had anything to declare. Looking as innocent as I could, I told him that I had just arrived from Zurich but that I had come from Germany and that I had nothing to declare. When he asked me to put my two cases on a table next to him and to open them I still felt completely confident that this would be merely a random check-up and that I would be allowed to exit the hall quickly. Not surprisingly, the camera in its brand new shiny leather casing attracted their immediate attention. And when I stated that this was my own personal property which I had just bought during my Christmas holiday and that the invoice for it was in my wallet they insisted on me handing the wallet to them. The invoice was indeed there, evidencing the purchase but then the officer pulled another piece of paper out of the wallet which was the original note from Jose, describing the type of camera he wanted and mentioning also the down payment of £50. How foolish of me not to have destroyed this paper after the actual purchase. With such hard evidence against me I had no choice but to admit my wrongdoing.

I was asked to hand over my passport which one of the officers took away to an adjacent office. To my horror I was then informed that my labour permit was being cancelled and that I would have to face a magistrate who would not only decide on the penalty payable but who would also rule whether or not my labour permit would be reinstated. In any case, the camera was being confiscated and my passport would be handed over to the Court Authorities. A car would take me shortly to a courtroom in Hounslow where I would be detained until the magistrate was ready to hear my case. Memories of my failed border crossing at Creuzburg eight years earlier were suddenly revived.

Unlike the barred prison cell in Creuzburg, I was taken to a small room in the basement of the building which at least had a table and also a long bench with a woolly blanket on top of it. A male warden, after first accompanying me to the cloakroom, brought me a bowl of soup with some bread and a glass of water and informed me that my case would be heard first thing the next morning.

I guess you had a very restless night with so much of your professional future at stake now. Losing the camera was probably the least of your worries.

It was indeed a restless night. Above all, I could not get over it that I had been so foolish not to have destroyed Jose's note. After all, I was no longer a little schoolboy but had thought of myself as a seasoned adult with sufficient judgement and foresight to avoid pitfalls of this magnitude. I felt a real failure.

The following morning I was taken up to the courtroom and after having gone through the procedure of providing my personal identity data a uniformed policeman then informed the magistrate that I had already admitted my guilt to the customs officials. A few more questions followed regarding the purpose of my visit to the UK and I was then asked if I could name a guarantor in case I was unable to pay the fine to be imposed upon me. With my own financial resources just adequate to have covered my travel back to Glasgow, I knew that I would be unable to pay any fine myself.

Since I was not even sure if in addition to a fine the magistrate would revoke my labour permit, I saw no alternative but to name my employer as my guarantor. I gave the telephone number of the Personnel Department at the Glasgow Head Office to a black-robed gentleman in the courtroom. He left the room instantly but returned only a few minutes later with a piece of paper, handing it over to the magistrate.

In an almost paternal manner I was then told by the magistrate that I had acted very foolishly but that my employer had generously agreed to stand by me and to pay the penalty. It is hard to describe my relief.

I was dismissed without any further ado, from which I gathered that my labour permit had been reinstated. When the black-robed court official handed me back my precious passport I quickly flicked through the pages and to my great relief the original labour permit – Nr 363232 – had been reinstated on a new page. I was asked to collect my two pieces of luggage, minus the camera, and a car similar to the one that had brought me here the day before, drove me back to Heathrow Airport. My airline ticket to Glasgow/ Renfrew was now out of date but after a lot of pleading with a senior airline official and attributing my missed connection to some corrections needed for my entry papers, the official finally took pity on me and revalidated my ticket without any further charge.

During the flight back to Scotland I was plagued by all sorts of thoughts. Not only would I have to explain to my Spanish colleague that due to my thoughtlessness the camera had been lost, but moreover I would also have to pay him back the £50 which he had given me as a down payment. Then there was also the additional money my father had paid to complete the purchase in Freiburg. With all these obligations ahead my financial future looked rather bleak. However, the thought uppermost in my mind was how would the Company view my misdemeanour? They had very generously bailed me out at the Hounslow Court but would they now tell me to pack my bags and return to Germany? Would I even be allowed to rejoin their MEZ subsidiary in Freiburg?

What would my parents think about this misadventure? Even when the plane touched down at Renfrew Airport I was still utterly possessed by these questions.

I take it that in the end everything turned out alright?

Yes, Joseph, to my great relief it did.

Back at Makerston House my misadventure led to a stream of frivolous comments and jokes. Benji, also just back from his Christmas break, took the opportunity to tease me that I had now joined him as the second Makerstonian to be bailed out by the Company. My Spanish colleague took the loss of the camera surprisingly well. He readily admitted that if it had not been for him asking me for this favour in the first place the whole fiasco would never have arisen.

"Forget about paying me back the deposit," he added, "I am very sorry I got you into this and I sincerely hope that you are now not marred with an official criminal record."

Until that moment that possibility had never even crossed my mind but hearing it now made me think that this may well have happened. After all I had been in an official courtroom in front of a magistrate and fined for my misconduct.

I coped quite well with all this banter from my colleagues but what about the reception I was likely to get the next day at the Glasgow Head Office?

Properly attired and again donning my bowler hat I even caught an earlier train from Paisley just to make sure that I did not have to rush from Glasgow Station to the Head Office building in St Vincent Street as had been the custom in the past. This morning I walked sedately to ensure that I arrived at the offices in a composed and unhurried manner.

When entering the personnel manager's office, I expected him to tell me straight away to report to the upper senior management floor to learn about my fate, but to my surprise I was merely asked to sit down and provide a detailed account of what had happened. During our ensuing conversation, I even seemed to sense in his responses that the manager himself felt sorry for me that I had not succeeded in my intended 'good deed' for a fellow trainee.

"In a worldwide organisation like ours," he said, "many situations arise which in the end have to be dealt with in a pragmatic manner."

No word of instant return to Germany or dismissal from the Company and to crown it all he even suggested that it would not serve any good purpose to report this incident to my management back home in Freiburg. I felt like grabbing the man's hand to express my gratitude, but quickly decided that such a show of emotion would probably be judged as excessive by him. When I raised the question of whether or not I might now have a 'criminal record' in the UK he volunteered to seek advice from the Legal Department.

"You are the first case of this kind since I started in my job," he added, "but since the imposed fine has been paid, I suspect that your misdemeanour will not have lumbered you with a permanent criminal record."

I did not have the nerve to ask him how much the Company had in the end paid for my release.

I am truly amazed by the patrician style of management which, judging by what you have mentioned before, looks like a general hallmark of this Company.

That is a very fitting description, Joseph, and I regarded myself a lucky beneficiary of that benevolent and patrician attitude. I have to admit that it was decidedly different from the hierarchical and predominantly task-driven culture which prevailed in the Freiburg offices and which at the time I myself had embraced without any questioning. Here, although it was also very much a commercial enterprise, it displayed an almost paternal behaviour which expressed itself not merely in the provision of widespread employment, but also in so many generous contributions to the wider community as was so evident in Paisley. I felt sure that if the final arbiter over my recent misadventure had been the management of the Company's subsidiary in Freiburg, the outcome would have been less sympathetic. The personnel manager in the Glasgow Office was obviously aware of such 'cultural' differences when he suggested that there was no pressing reason to report this unfortunate episode to the Freiburg management.

Chapter 7

At the end of my 'interview' I was handed my training programme for the next six months which, to my surprise and delight, included a seven-week spell in London. Firstly I was to spend six weeks in the Company's large warehouse on the Great West Road in London. This was the main distribution centre for customers in the south of the UK and my assigned task was to take customers' orders by telephone and to deal with queries and complaints. Joerg, the fellow trainee from Switzerland, was to accompany me on this assignment and details of our pre-booked accommodation would be given to us in due course. And then there was an additional surprise waiting for me. After completing my time at the warehouse I was to spend another week in London to attend a Leadership and Management Course at the Tack Organisation in Longmoore Street. Taking a closer look at the programme I noticed that a booking for the week starting 6 July had already been made for me at the Corah Hotel, the very same place I had stayed in when I first arrived in the country in April the previous year. When I mentioned this coincidence to the manager he admitted that the Company had been using this hotel for some years now for visitors and staff from overseas and Head Office personnel. I wondered if the friendly Irish lady at the reception desk would still be there.

Considering that I had entered the Head Office building that morning in fear of instant dismissal, the programme now revealed to me looked like a belated Christmas present. Moreover, this programme now also meant that before heading for London I would be spending the next few months in a variety of Head Office departments and thus remain domiciled at Makerston House. This was particularly pleasing as it would give me the opportunity to see more of Elaine and to find out if my personal interest and feelings for her would meet with a positive response. I still found it difficult to believe that an attractive young woman of her age and upbringing had not been pursued by a string of local suitors.

On my return to Makerston House I felt so elated that evening that, in spite of my precarious financial situation, I declared the house bar open at my expense. And my fellow trainees did not need much encouragement to make use of that offer.

As to be expected, they all wanted to hear in some detail as to how the Head Office management had reacted to my folly. Was I sent up to the fourth floor? They were surprised when they heard that the whole matter had been dealt with by the personnel manager.

"At least I was sent up to the fourth floor," interjected Benji, "when they bailed me out at Madrid Airport."

"Yours was a historical misfortune with political ramifications," I replied, "which clearly attracted attention at a higher management level. Mine was probably looked upon as a silly misdemeanour which did not deserve to pass a director's desk."

I decided that at this early stage of our still fragile relationship it would be best not to divulge anything to Elaine, although I was sure that on any further visits to Makerston House, or at the still-pending party at her own home, my fellow trainees would find it difficult not to indulge in some frivolous talk about my experience with the British judiciary system.

The new year had also brought some changes at Makerston House. Two of my colleagues, having completed their Scottish training, did not return after the Christmas break. One of them had taken up a junior management role in his home country, Brazil, and the other one had become a full-time employee in one of the Glasgow Head Office departments which no longer entitled him to reside at Makerston House.

There was, however, a newcomer, once again from the Company's Swiss subsidiary, which was located in the German-speaking part of that country. He introduced himself as Walter. Fortunately the German spoken by my two Swiss fellow trainees was much more understandable than what I had encountered when meeting Swiss people in the past. However, the English spoken by my two Swiss colleagues was so accomplished that we conversed in English most of the time. My Swiss colleague, Joerg, admitted that he had already been informed about a spell at the London warehouse and was pleased to learn now who his companion would be.

The opening session to my training programme at the

Glasgow Head Office proved to be of great interest. It gave me a deeper insight into the worldwide spread of this Company and the enterprising spirit of its management. I found it particularly fascinating to learn more about the humble beginnings of what, within a relatively short space of time, became what one can describe as a 'Thread Empire', employing over 50,000 people worldwide, and becoming the largest industrial enterprise in the UK. It was interesting to learn that once again the deprivations of war had led enterprising humans to overcome the lack of vital raw materials with alternative solutions. Had it not been for the cessation of silk supplies from the Continent due to the Napoleonic blockade of the UK, the Coats brothers might never have developed threads based on cotton imported from the USA through Liverpool. The industrial revolution in England also provided new machinery for spinning and twisting which furthered this development, and when eventually the household sewing machine became widely available, the Company was on course for a rapid expansion. The merger with the local competitor Clark finally resulted in a commercial colossus with Paisley being its industrial hub.

When overseas countries started to impose import bans or high duties, the Company set up many overseas manufacturing sites or purchased existing local enterprises, a policy mainly followed in Western Europe which, as was specially pointed out to me, led to the acquisition also of the MEZ AG in Freiburg.

Excuse me for interrupting you, Wolfgang, but are you telling me that your training programme for the next few months concentrated mainly on learning about the origins and the worldwide spread of the Company?

Not, not at all, but prior to continuing my training in a variety of Head Office departments I was most grateful that my initial week in the Secretariat Department had provided me not only with a historical insight into this Company but it had also boosted my pride in being part of such an enterprising organisation. This pride of belonging seemed to be a feature amongst all the members of staff I was to meet in the weeks to come.

The different Overseas Departments, designated by letters of the alphabet, the Estate Management and the Finance, Planning and Publicity Sections, provided fresh mental stimulus on a daily basis. As the weeks went by I began to feel that I had become part of that body of bowler-wearing men streaming each morning from Glasgow Central Station to their offices in the city.

A few days after my return from Germany and the debacle at London Airport I finally plucked up the courage to telephone Elaine. I thought an invitation to the cinema would test her willingness for an evening out just for the two of us. I remembered from my earlier days, when my mentor Andrew had taken me to the Paisley cinema to improve my understanding of English, that the audience consisted quite often of young couples who clearly regarded a visit to the cinema as a respectable form of entertainment. To my delight, Elaine was instantly in favour.

"I am sure," she said, "my mother will let me use her car on Thursday evening when she normally does her books and I will come to Makerston House to collect you."

It certainly left me with the feeling that our relationship was moving in the right direction.

The film, *Path of Glory*, was not really the right background to kindle a simmering romance, but on our way home Elaine assured me that she had very much enjoyed our first joint outing and that we should repeat it at the next possible opportunity, maybe with a visit to her favourite seaside place called Largs.

It was a day in early February when I returned from the Glasgow Head Office that my fellow trainee Jose met me at the door of Makerston House begging me to come quickly into the lounge to see the evening news on the television. With a solemn voice the BBC newsreader reported that the plane carrying the whole Manchester United football team had crashed at Muenchen-Riem Airport and that it was feared that there were a high number of fatalities. Apparently, the plane, on its way back from Portugal, had made a stopover for refuelling in Munich. but had then encountered severe wintery conditions on take-off.

For all of us, whether British or foreigners, the Manchester football team was the embodiment of top-class football with admirers from right round the globe. To me, this sad news had the additional impact that it had all happened in Munich and at Riem Airport from where my friend Walter and I once flew off on a memorable trip to Salzburg.

When I arrived the next morning at the Glasgow offices the Muenchen-Riem disaster was very much a topic of conversation throughout the building, particularly as by then further information had become public that 21 people had lost their lives, amongst them seven players of the Manchester United team. It had already come to my attention that the Scots were very proud of their own football teams, but the Munich disaster seemed to have produced an outpouring of sympathy for their southern compatriots which I found very laudable.

It must have been this tragic event which prompted me to attend a match between two of the leading Scottish teams. The match was to be played at the Ibrox Stadium and my Swiss colleague, Joerg, who was a keen football enthusiast, readily agreed to join me.

It must have been a very important match because large crowds had built up outside the entrance gate trying to get through a row of turnstiles. Once inside, the huge stadium looked packed with spectators and noisy exchanges amongst the opposing club supporters had already started before the teams had even appeared on the pitch.

Joerg and I decided to seek a place in the middle of the terraces which was standing-room only, and having seen the scramble of people trying to get into the stadium we also picked a place near the exit gate. By the time the two teams arrived on the pitch supported by the chanting of their supporters, Joerg and I were completely hemmed in on all sides by a particularly noisy group of young men.

The game commenced rather sluggishly, but after about

20 minutes and several missed goal-scoring opportunities which produced an almost groaning chorus from the spectators, one of the players suddenly displayed some really artistic footwork and after outrunning two of his opponents scored a magnificent and well-deserved goal.

There was a rapturous outburst of applause in the stadium but not where Joerg and I were standing. We both clapped enthusiastically to express our appreciation of a truly outstanding performance but regretted our action very swiftly. Two rows behind us a man started shouting abusive language and then tried to force his way to us by pushing the people in front of him. Within seconds, mayhem broke out with people on the ground and two bodies on top of me. Thankfully a stadium guard arrived quite quickly and we asked him to accompany us to the exit gate as we had no desire to stay on to see the end of this game. After this experience I decided to watch future Scottish football matches only on television.

Surely, Wolfgang, you must have been aware of the deep-rooted rivalry of some Glasgow teams and their supporters. When the people around you kept silent and the applause came from the other side of the stadium your and your friend's clapping was bound to lead to a hostile reaction from the supporters around you. You were lucky to get away without any injury.

Having previously only attended football matches at the Waldsee Stadium in Freiburg, where all spectators had always mingled freely around the stadium regardless of which team they supported, it had not occurred to me that here in Scotland sportive encounters of this kind could lead to something resembling tribal warfare. Later on, I also learnt that religious divisions added to the intensity of rivalry amongst spectators and teams particularly here in Glasgow. Well, Joseph it was yet another experience in a country which, while seemingly teeming with entrepreneurial spirit, generosity and tolerance, could also quickly lay bare its confrontational nature presumably nurtured by the historic tribalism of its society.

After having survived my encounter with Scottish football, my return to bowler-wearing visits to the Company offices in Glasgow not only transported me quickly back into the wider world of commerce and enterprise, but it gave me an unexpected opportunity to meet up with Elaine during many a lunchtime break. She had joined a Company with large offices in Sauchiehall Street, one of the main arterial roads in Glasgow, filled with bars, cafeterias and elegant boutique shops. Little did I know at this stage that Elaine's employer would one day play such a decisive role in our future relationship.

Our lunchtime meetings quickly helped to cement our relationship even further. At weekends I was introduced to a variety of relations and friends not only to test my social graces but more importantly to gauge the reaction of Elaine's wider family to this unexpected 'German Invasion'. To my relief, I passed these tests reasonably well, although I failed on my social graces when on one occasion I quite innocently responded positively to my host's suggestion to have a second helping of her delicious fish pie. When I was afterwards reminded that good manners demand that an offer for a second helping has to be turned down however hungry you are I felt absolutely dumbfounded. Here I was to compliment my host for the excellence of her cuisine by accepting her offer for a second helping, when in reality I was only trapped into committing a social faux pas.

Whilst this particular incidence left me slightly confused, it was a mere bagatelle compared with an unfortunate blunder only a few weeks later.

The ever-growing relationship between Elaine and myself must have come to the notice of the Coats Director responsible for the Company's interests in Western Europe. He was also on very friendly terms with Dr Adam Mez in Freiburg.

The personnel manager appeared one day to hand me an envelope with a very formal-looking card inside inviting me and Elaine to come for dinner at the director's private home in Bridge of Weir.

Back at Makerston House my news only led to a prolonged and frivolous guessing game with the overriding conclusion that it means 'promotion or demotion'. Nobody offered any serious suggestions as to why the invitation also included Elaine except to imply that the director may want to see for himself how this first German post-war recruit had managed to capture the heart of a Scottish girl.

Elaine was thrilled when I informed her about the invitation and offered to borrow her mother's car for the short journey to Bridge of Weir which, she added, was full of splendid grand houses.

The make or break day arrived. Elaine looked most alluring in her chequered dress and with a bunch of flowers at the ready we made our way to Bridge of Weir. Our hosts must have heard the arrival of our car and were both standing in the doorway to welcome us. The house, with its many paintings of Scottish Highland scenes, exuded warmth and homeliness. And yet I could not rid myself of spells of nervousness. Why had we been invited? Was it merely another event to test my social graces?

The conversation flowed easily and my host's questions reminded me of the interrogations which I had become so accustomed to during my sales training in Scotland. Yet I was constantly on edge in case the unfortunate episode at London Airport would be mentioned. My childhood days during the war and the immediate post-war years seemed to be of special interest to our hosts and, as to be expected, they did not hide their curiosity in wanting to hear more about how Elaine and I had come together.

I wish to add at this stage, Joseph, that I had thought that my level of competence in the English language was more than adequate to deal with all situations in one's daily life. But was it a sudden flush of nervousness caused by the previous reprimand I had received on this matter or just a slip of the tongue, I shall never know. When after completing my main course of the meal our hostess asked if I wanted another helping, I now knew that I had to decline it which I did.

Elaine's face suddenly looked slightly tortured with

embarrassment and our hosts across the table broke into what looked more like an amused grin. What had I done this time? Thanking our hostess and adding that I was "fed up" clearly demonstrated that there were still considerable gaps in my understanding of the intricacies of the English language.

At least our hosts saw the humorous side of my linguistic slip up. The rest of the evening passed by very harmoniously with even Elaine looking more relaxed again.

On our drive back to Makerston House I had expected Elaine to scold me for my silly mistake, but to my surprise no more was said about it. Instead she informed me that her mother had decided to hold the promised house party for the Makerston boys, as she called them, on the following Saturday and that I should establish how many of them would be coming.

Back at Makerston House, with several of my colleagues still having a lively time in the house bar, I had no choice but to give a resume of the 'High Level' invitation. Initially I had not intended to mention my linguistic blunder, but after downing a couple of late night drinks myself, I let it slip out, causing a roar of laughter amongst my fellow Makerstonians. My mentor Andrew found it particularly amusing. The general consensus of this alcohol-fuelled gathering was that my visit to Bridge of Weir was unlikely to lead to a promotion and that I should make the most of my friendship with Elaine to learn more about the finer points of the English language.

When before departing I mentioned the invitation to a

house party at Elaine's home for the coming Saturday, there were shouts of approval from literally all persons present. Knowing the size of Elaine's home I had quietly hoped that some of my colleagues would decline or be otherwise engaged on that day, but that was now not to be the case.

I was very glad when eventually I reached the calm and comfort of my own room. It certainly had been a day to remember.

Winter still held a firm grip on the country and by the time it came to party day at Elaine's home, heavy snowfalls had brought public traffic to a near standstill. However, two courageous taxi drivers responded to our call to collect us from Makerston House and promised to do their best to get our group of six to Elderslie, not far from the Ferguslie Mills. As we approached the village I pointed out to our driver that our destination was the house at the very top of the highest elevation in the village.

"You were lucky I got you this far," he said. "From here on you have to use your own legs."

When we saw the steepness of the snow-covered road leading up to the house we could instantly understand the driver's refusal to go any further.

The stone-built house with a quaint-looking turret had the welcoming name of 'Sunnyside', although on this day 'Snowyside' would have been more appropriate. Elaine and her mother, plus their poodle dog, greeted us at the door, but instead of being asked to enter the house Elaine's mother handed me a key to the garage door.

"Gentlemen," she said with a big smile on her face, "I

am sure you would not mind clearing the snow from our driveway before we start the party. The shovels are in the garage and with so many of you here the job will no doubt be completed very quickly."

One of my fellow Makerstonians gave me a nudge and whispered, "This lady does not miss an opportunity if she sees one."

The snow clearing was completed very quickly and once inside the house we soon restored our frozen hands at a roaring fire in the large lounge. For several of my fellow Makerstonians from overseas countries, this was the first time that they had set foot in a private Scottish home and Elaine's mother revelled in providing an insight into the Scottish way of life. Stories about her travels with Elaine to several Continental countries and also England, and her ability to engage easily with every single one of our group, quickly demonstrated that she was a lady with wide-ranging interests and well-rounded views on a multitude of topics. At the same time, it did not require much imagination to see that this was also a lady who would not readily take 'no' for an answer and who also expected her daughter to toe the line.

The dining-room table was laden with a wide range of Scottish delicacies, many of them home baked. It was at this stage that two of my colleagues could not refrain from bringing up my unfortunate blunder at the recent dinner at the home of our company director. Although it was all said in a jocular manner and supported by grinning faces all around me, it made me feel uncomfortable because I knew that my colleagues would probably use this party to tease me also over my ill-fated return from Germany at new year. And lo and behold, they did.

I could tell from the expression on the faces of Elaine and her mother that they were thinking, what else is he hiding from us? Thankfully my fellow Makerstonians soon realised that their loose talk had caused a rather embarrassing situation for me, and they quickly turned my misfortune in London into a tale of true comradeship for a fellow trainee. Nevertheless, I did not escape the critical observations of Elaine and her mother that I could have easily endangered my whole future career.

From the lounge window we could see that traffic was again flowing easily on the main road giving us hope that we could get public transport services back to Makerston House.

All my colleagues expressed their genuine thanks for the hospitality extended to us and on finally parting, one of them jokingly suggested that if the house gets snowed under again, phone Makerston House. Little did he know that our hostess was the kind of lady who could easily take him up on his flippant offer.

The freak winter conditions soon gave way to spring displaying itself in an unexpected plethora of colours and lush greens. This was my first experience of Scotland in springtime and I was genuinely surprised by the diversity of the flora in a country which one had always regarded as being located on the uppermost northern fringes of Europe.

At weekends, Elaine and her mother introduced me to what appeared to be an ever-increasing number of members of their own wider family, plus school friends and acquaintances, but on a few rare occasions, when Elaine could loan her mother's car, the two of us could escape to her favourite seaside place Largs with its famous Nardini ice cream parlour. It was on one of these trips that we both confessed to each other that this was more than a mere friendship.

Is that the best you can do to tell me that you had finally declared your love for her?

You are right to take me up on this, Joseph, but with my upbringing I have always found it quite difficult to display feelings very freely and certainly not spontaneously. In fact, I had felt for some time that this restraint is also a widespread feature amongst people in Scotland, except maybe at football matches as I had found out to my own discomfort.

Chapter 8

With some of my fellow Makerstonians having reached the end of their training programme and returning to their home countries or taking up positions in other overseas markets, several new trainees had arrived, one of which was Rudi, a fellow employee of the Mez AG in Freiburg, but working in the Company's large spinning mill in a place called Bräunlingen in the Black Forest.

Our newcomers embraced the Makerston House way of life very quickly and turned into lively participants of our now less-frequent house parties. Their popularity amongst our core lady guests remained undiminished. On this latest occasion, Sylvia brought along another young lady who was also one of Elaine's longstanding friends. Her name was Helga. I learnt later that her father had been a senior executive of the Coats Company in Mexico, but that he was killed in a tragic road accident which had involved the whole family. Not only did Helga lose her father, but in the aftermath of the accident, which had left all the other family members injured or traumatised at the scene, local inhabitants had quickly appeared to rob the victims of their jewellery and other valuable possessions. It sounded a heartbreaking story, more the material for a horror film.

The date for my departure to London came closer and closer and Elaine and I used every available opportunity to share each other's company. During the week, this consisted mainly of meetings in cafeterias during our lunchtime breaks in Glasgow, and rarely a weekend passed without Elaine's mother organising day trips to beauty spots in the Highlands. When I admitted that I had never been to Edinburgh it was immediately marked down as a 'must' for the next outing, with the additional promise to take me there again in August for the famous Tattoo.

At one time my posting to London had looked a very appealing part of my training programme, but I was beginning to wonder if such a long separation might cool down our now-blossoming relationship. How would she take the latest additional news that after London and an additional training week at the Company's wool processing mill at Darlington I would only spend a short spell back at the Glasgow Offices before returning to Germany at the end of July? Will that be the end of it all?

I was rather surprised about my early return date to Freiburg as I remembered quite clearly that during the original interview with Dr Mez a period of up to two years was mentioned, whereas now my programme seemed to finish after only 14 months.

The fact that the latest news also indicated that I was to return to Freiburg to take up a junior management role gave me at least the assurance that my training results so far had been judged favourably. I decided to sleep on this news for a few nights before putting Elaine fully into the picture, although deep down I felt such a postponement would merely give me restless nights and still no clear answers for the future.

It had by now become abundantly clear that Elaine would not entertain any ongoing relationship in which her mother's wellbeing and security was not properly protected. After all, after Elaine's father's tragic early death, her mother's determined effort to carry on with the insurance agency business and make it flourish had instilled in Elaine a deep sense of gratitude for the sheltered and well-rounded upbringing she had enjoyed as a result of her mother's efforts.

You certainly have a hard nut to crack here, Wolfgang, and no one to help you either.

To be honest it felt more like a raw egg about to fall off my spoon.

The letter from the Personnel Department duly arrived advising Joerg and me of the pre-booked accommodation near our next training base, plus railway tickets and even a detailed description of the final stages by underground to a station called Osterley. Once again I could not hide my admiration for the way in which the Company organised all our movements. When I mentioned this to Joerg however his mind was clearly occupied with other matters.

"I telephoned my parents yesterday," he said, "who told me that a summons had arrived for my 1958 army service and that non-attendance would result in a fine. The army service would only last for a few days and basically they really only want to make sure I still know how to handle my carbine rifle which I keep in my cupboard. Now this summons falls right in the middle of our programme in London and I had really intended to make the most of our time there."

I had heard some vague stories before about able-bodied Swiss men all keeping a rifle at their homes, but I had never heard about them being summoned for army manoeuvres or rifle practice, as I and probably many people had never thought of Switzerland as actually having an army. When I mentioned this to Joerg he replied, "One of my more illustrious countrymen once said, Switzerland does not have an army, Switzerland is an army."

Quite a striking statement I thought, and with over 200 years of peace behind them their system seems to work.

When Joerg went to speak to the personnel manager the following day, I was not at all surprised to learn that rather than have the training programme interrupted, the Company would pay the fine. According to the Swiss Consul, the payment of the fine by a third party would not have any adverse judicial consequences for Joerg when he returned to his home country All this brought back to me my own predicament not so long ago and also the rescue of Benji from the clutches of the Spanish military. At the time the personnel manager had so aptly wrapped it up in his memorable phrase, "In a worldwide organisation like ours, many situations arise which in the end have to be dealt with in a pragmatic manner."

I wondered what pearls of wisdom he would also have to deal with the more complicated world of international human relations.

After first writing a letter to my parents advising them of my return at the end of July, I finally plucked up enough courage to put Elaine fully into the picture. I was absolutely astounded how calmly she took it all in. No expression of sadness, no tears. Had our romance been just a sham after all, or was this the way the 'ice maidens of the North' faced up to difficult situations?

I was about to suggest that the two of them come over to Freiburg to meet the family and experience a German Christmas when Elaine pre-empted my intended proposal by suggesting that I might like to come to Scotland for the Christmas and new year break.

What choice did I have? I agreed readily, but it completely defeated my intention of giving Elaine at least a taste of German life and to find out if she could possibly adapt to it. It suddenly occurred to me that the colourful carnival season in February might be a strong enough lure to bring Elaine to Freiburg. And so it was.

With now only specific dates to be set for our visits, the looming return to Germany did in the end not appear to be the end of our romantic journey, in fact it was only just the beginning.

The day finally arrived. Joerg and I had to clear our rooms because new arrivals were expected at Makerston House. On our long train journey down south we had ample time to map out a plan for all the London attractions we were going to visit. It became obvious very quickly that my Swiss colleague's suggestions were not constrained by any financial shortcomings. He told me that he also wanted to contact an old school friend who now worked for a publishing firm in London. That was good news because it would give me some time to myself. Joerg was by nature quite a lively and pleasure-seeking character and, unlike myself, not really fond of quiet moments.

Thanks to the detailed instructions from the Personnel Department we reached Osterley station (which turned out to be above ground) without any trouble and our new landlord's terrace house was only a short walk away.

Over the years, the Company had clearly gone to considerable length to find good lodgings for their trainees and visiting staff. A smartly dressed middle-aged lady opened the door, but before letting us enter she politely asked us to let her see the Company letter with the booking details.

"From which country do you two hail from?" she asked.

When we told her Germany and Switzerland, she admitted that previous lodgers had either been Scottish or English or from countries much further away.

After being introduced to the lady's husband who tried to test his German on us by a hearty *"Willkommen in London"* we were shown to our rooms on the upper floor. Although small, the rooms had a comfortable feel to them, they were light and the beds looked comfortable. We were left to ourselves to decide who would take which room.

Joerg, being considerably taller than me, had already noticed that the bed in one of the rooms was longer than the other one which settled the choice of rooms without any further debate.

When asked about our preferences for breakfast we both

expressed our preference for a simple Continental type with rolls, butter, jam and coffee which seemed to go down well with our landlady. After all, so much easier and less costly than a full, cooked offering of a traditional English breakfast. It all seemed to settle down very well, except that there was no telephone.

The Company warehouse on the Great West Road was only a short walk away from our lodgings. The manager turned out to be a Scotsman who had previously worked at the TCA Distribution Centre at the Ferguslie Mill. This immediately ensured a good rapport with him. I had expected that both Joerg and I would be following the same training programme, but we were now told that I would be working at a desk in the adjacent office, whereas Joerg would be assigned to the warehouse to assist the regular staff with the physical preparation of customers' orders, stock replacement and dealing with the carriers who delivered the goods to the customers' premises.

I, on the other hand, was expected to demonstrate my communication skills by taking orders from clients over the telephone, by dealing with enquiries and complaints and on top of which I was also to maintain contact with the official Company Sales Representatives. When I heard all this I really felt I had drawn the shorter straw. This after all was not Scotland with little hamlets and market towns dotted over a vast area, but a huge metropolis, surrounded by a densely populated hinterland. On top of which I had already noticed that people seemed to talk so much faster.

"You will not be on your own," the manager added, "and

in any case for the first few days you will be the understudy to one of our two order clerks."

During our lunchtime breaks we soon became to know the whole warehouse team very well and each member came up with loads of different suggestions as to what we should do with our free time whilst in London.

After two days of listening in and filling out order sheets for my mentor, I was given my own desk, my telephone line was hooked up to the small central exchange board operated by a young lady at the rear of our office and it was now a question of sink or swim.

The first call came within minutes and I expected someone to express their requirements for our products by simply quoting product numbers or the length of zip fasteners required. But on this occasion the lady at the other end of the line must have been a recent newcomer to the country as her strongly accented English was very difficult to understand. We both struggled along for some time and in the end I could not help myself to ask her where she came from.

"I have only recently arrived from Athens," she said, "but our business here in London was started by my grandfather after the First World War."

Yet another reminder of the magnetic power this country seems to possess to attract and to embrace people from different cultures and backgrounds and in providing a safe haven for people in distress from many different parts of the world. It brought back memories of my earlier encounter with the Asian business people in Leicester and how they had become an accepted feature of the whole local community. What did these people think, when they initially set out on their journey to this country? For me the whole concept of Empire and Commonwealth had only been a topic covered in a few pages of my earlier German school history books and then often with critical undertones of exploitation and suppression. As I discovered with time, these immigrants did not look upon themselves as intruders but more like family members who wanted to seek their fortune at the hub of the Empire. To them, unlike myself, it was clearly not a journey into the unknown.

There were instances when one became aware of a 'them and us' attitude amongst the indigenous population, but then I myself had gone through a phase of mild discrimination and been sidelined after arriving in Freiburg as a German refugee from the East. I could not imagine Germany ever being able to equal this country's capacity to absorb people from all corners of the world. The very recent history of the Final Solution was an instant forceful reminder of my own country's limited capacity to live with and tolerate diversity of the kind I was now witnessing around me here.

I am astonished you and your Swiss friend have not started yet to explore the sites and landmarks of London. If I remember correctly on you train journey down from Glasgow you two had already made a plan of which attractions you regarded as 'must be seen'.

We had indeed a large number of places on the original 'must be seen' list, but our new colleagues from the warehouse team with their superior local knowledge made our original plan look rather amateurish. Visiting the zoo, the Tower, the wax museum and planetarium and even the Tate Gallery was judged by some of them as a typical tourist programme and if we wanted to get a real taste of their beloved city we should spend an evening in Soho's Chinese quarters and visit some of the historic ale houses down the river like Samuel Pepys. We did not need much persuading to add their suggestions to our list.

Joerg added to this list also that his Swiss school friend had invited us to a dinner at the Swiss Centre in Leicester Square on a date still to be agreed.

The nearby Osterley station provided easy and quick access to the heart of the city and with Joerg being decidedly more anxious than me to spend every free moment on exploring this buzzing metropolis, we made rapid progress in ticking off our targeted star attractions. The planetarium was one of the most memorable places and I could have spent hours watching this miraculous presentation of our universe. I felt as overawed by it as I did when visiting the architectural marvel of St Paul's Cathedral.

My job in the warehouse office turned out to be much busier than I had expected, particularly as there were three of us dealing with incoming calls. The business was clearly thriving. I got more and more accustomed to the fast-talking customers and my requests for "could you repeat this please" became fewer every week.

Until now I had written all my training notes in German, but I now realised I had to make a serious effort to master also writing in English to keep my relationship with Elaine alive. I struggled with my first few letters. I could have asked Joerg to correct some of the crassest grammar and spelling mistakes but did not think it right to share with him my very personal feelings for my girlfriend. In her responses, Elaine never made any reference to any mistakes, on the contrary she complimented me on the progress I was making.

The end of our London training period approached so quickly that we did not manage to complete our wish list. With the end of June upon us, parks and gardens were in full bloom and one got the feeling of being in a green city decorated with grand buildings and cathedrals, endless streams of tourists and a constant hum of traffic, almost a form of background music.

Little did I know at this stage that many years later London would become my own place of work.

Joerg's ongoing training programme required him to return to Glasgow, whereas I was now due to attend this rather mysterious week-long Leadership and Management course in Longmoore Street. I still found it an extraordinary coincidence that I should now find myself in the same hotel again which had accommodated me on my very first day in this country over 15 months ago. Will that friendly Irish lady still be at the reception desk?

On 4 July, during our lunch break the manager called all the staff together and after a rather complimentary farewell speech all of us were offered a small glass of sherry to cheer us on our way. After all these weeks, we both felt that we had really become part of this team and we were grateful for their support and friendship.

Since the Company had only booked me into the Corah Hotel from Sunday onwards I stayed on in our lodgings until then, but Joerg was keen to get back to Makerston House and rushed off quickly after our farewell at the warehouse to catch the afternoon train to Glasgow. Somehow I wished I could have gone with him to have some more time with Elaine before my final return to Germany.

Finally, on Sunday I made my way to the Corah Hotel, only to find that the friendly Irish lady was no longer working there and also that the doorman had changed. I have heard it said before that one should always be prepared not to expect places to remain unchanged since in the majority of cases it would only result in disappointment. And that was certainly the case here. There was a different atmosphere to this hotel now. Still, the room was clean and comfortable and the staff was friendly and helpful but it all felt different.

This feeling of difference soon manifested itself in a form I had least expected. Whilst having a quick drink at the hotel bar I was joined by a well-dressed middle-aged gentleman who in a most friendly manner wanted to know what had brought me to London. After only a few exchanges he offered me another drink which I accepted. With that he moved his bar stool even closer to mine and I suddenly felt his hand probing into my trouser pocket, stroking my thigh. I quickly grabbed his wrist to get his hand away from me and with leaving his offered drink untouched I immediately retired to my room.

Was he also staying in this hotel? Would he be there for breakfast tomorrow morning? Was he just an evening visitor looking for like-minded individuals at the hotel bar? As it happened I never saw him again, but the encounter at the bar left me with a strong feeling of unease. What made the man think that I might possibly be a willing partner? Do I look the type? To be honest, Joseph, I was quite shaken by this episode.

The course at the Tack Organisation was attended mainly by people of my own age group, representing a wide cross section of different industries, ranging from banks to steel manufacturers, the motor car industry, shipbuilding, transport and even timber importers to mention just a few. Under the critical eyes of our tutors there was a lot of role-playing amongst us students, with some study cases requiring thorough analysis and in the end unanimous agreement. Sometimes it was the speed of sound decision-taking, techniques of interviewing, the role of advertising and a host of related aspects of day to day company management. Then there was the very topical and allegedly extremely complex issue of relationships with unionised workforces, a subject which seemed to be of special interest to my fellow students from the steel motorcar and shipbuilding industry. Listening to the debates and having been told during the early days of my training in Glasgow that Coats was one of the country's largest employer of people, I began to think that on this particular subject I must have missed out on something since during my training in the large mills in Paisley I never became aware of any organised movement to question or confront the management on matters of working conditions or social welfare. Listening now to my fellow students, and hearing especially about the strength of the Union movement amongst the workforces on the River Clyde, I could only conclude that the Coats management style was already ahead of other industries in making it unnecessary for the workforce both in the mills and offices to seek the settlement of grievances by disruptive unionised actions.

It turned out to be a most interesting week, with a few after hours get-togethers in a nearby pub often prolonging the already very animated discussions during the daytime hours.

Chapter 9

During the week, a letter arrived from the personnel training officer with a detailed programme for the rest of my stay in the country. I was to travel on 12 July to Darlington to spend a week at the Company's wool processing mill after which I was to return to Makerston House and report to K Department in Glasgow for the remainder of my stay. A flight to Basel had been booked for 31 July and the ticket would be given to me in due course. In Darlington, I would have lodgings with one of the Company's employees whose address was enclosed, and to complete it all the letter contained the rail vouchers from London to Darlington and then from Darlington to Glasgow.

The letter was just another example of the attention to detail and general paternal care which the Company expended on their young management trainees. It provided normally a sense of comfort and security, but on this occasion it felt more like a notice of eviction with 31 July now firmly written into the calendar.

The train journey to Darlington turned out to be longer than I had expected, but it gave me a welcome opportunity to write not only a letter to Elaine but also a series of postcards with well-known London landmarks to my old friends Walter and Klaus, my own family, the Tischer family in Luebeck and Unkel Peter and Aunt Lotte in Hamburg. The sudden urge to make them all aware of my stay in this world metropolis must have been driven by the belief that this would probably be the only time I would ever have this opportunity.

On arrival at Darlington Railway Station posters and placards made sure that the traveller was aware of the pioneering role Darlington had played in the history of rail travel. During my short taxi ride to my new lodgings it became obvious that this was very much a centre of heavy engineering and industrial enterprises, very different from Paisley with its distinctive cotton-processing mills and tenement houses, in contrast to the rows of terraced houses I was passing now. My new landlords lived in a larger house at the end of one of these terraces. Mr Barlow was a wool buyer and I soon learnt that he even travelled to Australia from time to time to purchase high-quality merino wool fleeces. When he showed me a copy of my programme for the week it became clear that this was not going to be a holiday. It was my first training schedule where each day was broken down into hourly sessions covering every single stage from wool sorting to the sales and export offices for the finished products. There seemed to be no space left to develop any personal contact with my mentors. And so it turned out. After an early breakfast, Mr Barlow asked me to join him in his car to start my week's labour. Firstly, I reported to the site manager, who after briefly mentioning that I was the first German to receive training at his plant, simply wished me good luck and from his office window pointed me to a shed-like building where he said I would get my hands dirty.

According to my programme, the training in this shed

was to be for four hours, the longest single session during the whole week. When entering I could already detect an unusual tang in the air. It reminded me of my childhood days on the farm way back in Mecklenburg.

The shed was filled with neatly rolled up sheep fleeces and in the middle of the room were large tables where several men in overalls were busy unrolling these fleeces and seemingly randomly pulling them apart into separate heaps of wool.

The foreman, after a brief welcome, sized me up and asked me to slip into an overall he had picked from a cabinet.

"That young man over there will take care of you for the next few hours," he said.

I have to admit that my four hours in this department turned out to be the most interesting ones during my whole week at the Darlington plant. And the site manager was right too. The fleeces may have looked snug and clean, but my hands soon looked greasy and dirty. I had had no idea how many different wool qualities there were within one fleece, but under the guidance from my mentor I soon began to see where in a spread-out fleece the quality choices had to be made. I was quite fascinated by this rather basic sorting process and in the evening my new landlord, being a professional wool buyer, was only too anxious to tell me more about his own experiences, the bidding at auctions, visits to remote farms in Australia and the different qualities needed for our large range of wool yarns. It all struck me as being much more challenging and also exciting than buying those large bales of cotton piled up in the Ferguslie Mills in Paisley.

After this first day I was virtually passed each day from one department to another at one or two hour intervals, and when on Friday I finally arrived at the Sales and Export Department I felt quite drained and certainly ready for my journey back to Makerston House.

You have stayed remarkably silent, Wolfgang, on how over several weeks now you have managed to keep your romance with your Scottish Ice Maiden alive.

Yes, it prayed on my mind almost daily. The public telephone service proved to be very efficient and my letter writing had developed to a degree where one could almost describe it as a ritual, thankfully reciprocated by Elaine during my extended stay in London. It was merely the beginning of a flood of letters which for both of us became the binding glue of our relationship for quite some time.

Makerston House did not seem like the place of old. Several of my earlier fellow trainees had either gone back to their home countries or were on a section of their training programme that excluded their residence at the house. There were two newcomers from England and a young Scotsman, back from an overseas secondment. My fellow countryman Rudi seemed to have settled in very well and Joerg looked as if he was going to make Makerston House his life residence. Jose was still there, but told me that he was due to return to Spain at the beginning of September with the prospects of a senior position in the Fabra/Coats

140

Company. Benji also reported that he was approaching the end of his training and that he would be heading back to Chile sometime in September.

"I shall remind our Travel Department in due course not to book my flight via Madrid," he added. "Who knows what the Spanish military would do to me if they can get hold of me again."

I remember saying to him how strange it was that he made that fateful trip to Madrid to free himself of an unwanted relationship whereas I now have an unwanted departure date and a serious relationship.

Somehow, however, hearing now that some of my earliest fellow trainees were also due to return to their homes made my own rather imminent departure date look a little bit more bearable.

On Sunday I joined Elaine and her mother for a service at the Elderslie village church. To my relief, the liturgy had many features similar to the Lutheran Church and the vicar in his plain black tunic reminded me very much of Pastor Gallay way back in Rostock.

The afternoon, and indeed many of the remaining weekday evenings, were filled with visiting not only members of the wider family but also friends and acquaintances where I was not always sure whether they were distantly related or relationships grown out of Elaine's mother's flourishing insurance business. Whatever home we visited, I was truly made to feel welcome, which was slightly painful as it was really an occasion to say goodbye.

Once again I donned my height-enhancing bowler hat

on my final daily visits to the Glasgow offices and Elaine and I managed a few more lunchtime get-togethers at different Sauchiehall coffee shops.

Finally, on my last working day, the training manager handed me my airline ticket from Glasgow/Renfrew to Basel. And there it was in print: departure 30July. When I expressed surprise at being sent back on a Wednesday rather than travel the following Monday, which would have given me an extra weekend with Elaine, I was told that the newly opened direct flight between Glasgow and Basel only operated on a Wednesday.

All my fellow trainees always seemed to be quite elated when they received their instructions for returning to their home countries. Several of them had celebrated the news with throwing an evening house party. I could only say that I felt miserable and depressed and did not appreciate the well-meant teasing and jokes from my fellow Makerstonians. That evening, after having said my goodbye to Elaine and her mother, I felt more like leaving a home rather than returning to one.

When I telephoned my parents to let them know that my return was now final my mother, being possibly more sensitive to her children's moods than fathers normally are, observed already that my message was lacking the enthusiasm she had expected for such a joyous event.

On the flight to Basel, a gentleman passenger next to me tried to engage me in some conversation, but from my facial expression he must have realised very quickly that I really wanted to be left alone. Listening to this gentleman's story as to why he had to fly to Switzerland was of no interest to me when I had to ponder over serious problems affecting my own life.

I had already told my parents that I would take the train from Basel back to Freiburg and that there was no need to meet me at the airport. And so, finally during the afternoon of 30 July I arrived back at our apartment at No. 16, Merzhauserstrasse. The family was clearly pleased to see me back again and my mother in particular left no stone unturned to let me know that I had come home.

Brother Lothar had meanwhile become a qualified motor mechanic with the DKW-Audi Company, and Dietmar, now over 13 years old, was still enjoying the carefree life at school. My father was still in the same job with the German Post Office and according to my mother had become an ardent student of astrology which she herself regarded as a form of self-deception and abrogation of our Christian faith. Somehow, my father maintained that he could combine the two.

The following day I returned to the Mez AG offices to learn about my new responsibilities. Having worked in the Industrial Department before my departure to Scotland, I was very pleased to learn that I would now be the assistant manager of this department. As to be expected, many of my colleagues bombarded me with questions about my stay in Scotland.

It was only a week or so later that the Scottish gentleman whose presence I had always found to be rather mysterious during my apprenticeship days, called me into his office and invited me to join him and his wife the following Sunday for afternoon tea at their house in Herdern. Unlike the Merzhauserstrasse where we lived, Herdern was a part of Freiburg strewn with elegant villas and colourful gardens. As it turned out, Mr and Mrs Grant's house was not only elegant and spacious but also furnished in a way that left nobody in doubt about their Scottish origin. Mr Grant was clearly a keen practitioner of what he proudly declared as a Scottish invention, the game of golf.

To my embarrassment I had to admit that during all my time in Scotland I had never attempted to participate in this sport. I remembered that several of my Scottish and English fellow trainees at Makerston House had disappeared on dry weekends for a round of golf, as they described it, and which subsequently often provided material for animated discussions amongst them after their return to the House. I began to think now that I may have missed out on a vital aspect of Scottish life.

To my surprise, Mr Grant suggested that I might like to have a try on a nearby golf course. I had never heard of a golf course in the Freiburg region but I now learnt that the company Gütermann, a well-known manufacturer of silk threads located in the nearby village of Gutach, had their own private golf course. Mr Grant sounded confident that he could take me along as a guest and that I might enjoy a few practice rounds.

During the following weeks we did in fact make several visits to this secluded and beautifully maintained golf course and I was grateful for Mr Grant's efforts to teach me the basics of holding the club, swings and positioning of my feet and general posture. Like probably all beginners, I had a few lucky shots, but as I realised all too soon, luck alone is not enough in this game. In the years to come, I maintained an interest in this sport but failing to pursue it with the passion clearly needed to achieve a high standard, my skill level remained rather low. I also never quite lost the fear of causing serious damage to the greens when so many of my shots ended up with the golf ball rolling away followed or overtaken by a few square inches of turf.

I suppose as time passed by you settled into your new job and also reconnected with your old friends and fellow members of the European Youth Movement. Presumably that must have helped you to overcome or at least reduce your hankering for the life on the other side of the Channel?

Yes, it all helped, but somehow I did not feel completely at home any more. The countryside around Freiburg was as beautiful as ever, prized by tourists from all over the world, the University added a vibrant young atmosphere to the town and cultural events were of the highest standards, and yet I felt unsettled.

Before settling into my new job properly, the Company had granted me a few days leave to visit the EXPO 1958 in Belgium. It had some special significance as it was the first world exhibition after the war with Germany once again being a participant. It was a very uplifting experience with so many countries, some of which I had not even heard of, presenting themselves in imaginative pavilions and open air show areas. When I visited the German pavilion I was very impressed that the organising authority had chosen a famous quote from Martin Luther over the front entrance to the pavilion. "If the world were to perish tomorrow I would still plant my apple tree today." Quite symbolic I thought for a nation that not so long ago itself had stood on the verge of an abyss.

The outstanding showpiece of the event was that imposing Atomium, symbolising not only the new age of nuclear power but acting also as a reminder of its horrendous potential for destruction and its role in deepening the East–West divide.

Back in Freiburg I now realised fully that my industrial sales training in Leicester had been a very valuable experience. I could converse confidently with our industrial customers, although I have to admit a strong Swabian dialect was sometimes no less challenging than the often strange intonation of the English language by the Far Eastern managers and buyers amongst my customers in Leicester. My social life began to regain its momentum and letter writing to Scotland filled a large part of my spare time.

It must have been late October when to all our surprise my brother Lothar announced that he had signed a three-and-a-half-year contract to work for DKW/AUDI in Johannesburg.

Here was another family member going to an unknown destination and on top of it so far away that frequent return journeys would be out of the question. It would be many years later that I met up again with him and his wife Erika at their apartment in Johannesburg, but that is a story in itself.

Now with Lothar off to Africa and me already committed to spending Christmas in Scotland, that left only young Dietmar to share the festive days with our parents. I comforted myself with the thought that many parents would eventually find themselves in this situation, with children seeking fortune and new lives in far-flung places round the globe. I suspect that I and possibly my generation, who in the war and post-war years had seen the traditional family cohesion severely strained or destroyed, were more prepared to accept the volatility which had crept increasingly into the old family bonds.

Snow arrived early this year and the slopes of the Schauinsland mountains and cosy guest houses exuded once again their magnetic power to bring people of all ages out to test their skiing skills on the hill sides. It brought back memories of my initial attempts as a schoolboy to acquire the basic skills of this sport. Would I still have the confidence to descend to Freiburg via the infamous Kaltwasser run? Could I risk another broken leg, as had happened years back in Kufstein, now that I was a junior manager in a large industrial enterprise? The date for my departure to Scotland was also approaching fast. I decided therefore not to tempt fate and on my last descent to Freiburg, just before Christmas, I chose a gentle route back which, thanks to heavy snowfall the day before, enabled me to ski back almost to the front door of our home on the outskirts of the town.

Chapter 10

On 24 December I finally set off for Zurich again and after a trouble-free transit through London Airport I landed at Glasgow/Renfrew with Elaine and her mother and the dog waiting for me. Our separation of five months did not seem to have cooled down our feelings for each other. In fact, our embrace was even more passionate than I had dared to hope for.

This being my first ever Christmas outside Germany, I was quite curious to learn how Scottish families and the wider community celebrated this important date in the Christian calendar. I remembered that my earlier mentor, Andrew, had once mentioned that for many Scots the new year was the dominant annual event for celebrations and merriment. On our drive back from the airport I had already noticed that the Paisley town centre and shop windows were only modestly adorned with the traditional décor of the season. Quite a contrast to the colourful and lively Christmas market around the old minster in Freiburg and the festive appearance of many public and private buildings throughout the town.

Thankfully, Elaine's home displayed a very Christmassy spirit and appearance; not so different from the elaborate décor my mother used to create each year, even during the challenging post-war years in East Germany.

With my return journey firmly fixed for 4January, Elaine's mother had not wasted any time in organising an extensive visiting programme for the length of my stay. It struck me that Scottish people seem to use this time of the year for almost frenetic socialising. Or was it merely Elaine's mother trying to squeeze a maximum amount of it into the limited duration of my visit? On reflection, I think the latter was the case.

Having completed the round of visits to Elaine's grandmother, the homes of Sylvia and Helga in Paisley, the Allan family in Renfrew and family members in the neighbourhood, I remember very fondly our visit to the MacKellar Family in Greenock. They lived in a magnificent house on the Esplanade with nothing but the wide expanse of the River Clyde in front and the contours of the Scottish Highlands in the far distance. The family were most hospitable and the whole house seemed to radiate warmth and welcome to whoever entered there. They symbolised the proverbial Samaritan and I felt it a true privilege to have spent joyful hours with them.

The day of my departure was nearly upon us when I finally raised the subject of Elaine's visit to Freiburg. Could she get a week's leave in February? Letting her see and participate in the colourful and exuberant events of a German carnival, or Fasnet as it was called in the Freiburg region, might lead her to seeing my country as an interesting place in which to make friends and maybe even to settle down in. Such a visit would also give me at long last the opportunity to introduce Elaine to my parents.

Did you really think that a noisy carnival with presumably many occasions of overindulgence would set the right tone for encouraging a young girl to make life-changing decisions?

Wishful thinking is probably the best description for even entertaining such thoughts, Joseph. However, when Cupid's arrow strikes, it seems cold reasoning suddenly becomes overwhelmed by a wave of optimism which completely ignores the fact that this may be no more than an adrenalin-driven spout of self-delusion.

Experiencing a carnival however seemed to strike home with Elaine and she saw no problem in getting the necessary leave from the office.

"It may only be a week," she added, "but if that includes the main procession on Rosenmontag it would be a wonderful experience. I might even bring a fancy costume for the occasion."

With the prospects of another reunion only a few weeks away, it was a rather casual farewell at the airport with the promise that I would hear soonest about the date and time of her arrival at Basel Airport.

My parents were really excited by the news and prospect of coming face to face with this mysterious young girl from the north who was clearly more than just a fleeting relationship. My mother, in typical fashion, began to wonder whether our modest and old-fashioned apartment would be a suitable abode for Elaine, particularly after she had listened to me describing Elaine's own home in Scotland.

The next letter from Elaine was already providing details

of her flight to Basel and moreover the duration of her stay would also include the Rosenmontag.

The scene was set for a very important milestone in my life. Will I be able to convince her that life in Germany, and in particular in this picturesque region of the country, could be the basis for our life together?

As happens so often, February can be an unpredictable month and 1959 was no exception. Basel Airport at this time did not have the feel of an international airport, compared with Zurich. When there was an announcement that the London plane would be delayed and that further details would be given in due course strange thoughts went through my mind. I am not normally superstitious, but was this an omen?

Finally, after several hours delay, a smartly dressed young lady stepped out of the exit door with a suitcase which seemed quite excessive for a week's visit. I was about to give her a hearty welcome embrace when I was told that I had not shaved. I was quite taken aback by this remark and it made me realise that in any future relationship with Elaine her attention to appearance and etiquette will clearly play an ever-present role in our daily life. It is quite amazing how a small and completely unexpected remark of this kind can trigger off many other questions. Was my mother right when she expressed her fears that our modest apartment might not come up to Elaine's expectation?

Thankfully, during our short train journey back to Freiburg, and with a department all to ourselves, the somewhat cool reception at the airport was quickly put behind us and my mind reverted to plans for the coming week. Maybe a visit to Mr and Mrs Grant who, after all, seemed to have settled down very well in Freiburg, could provide some assistance to 'sell' the attractions of life in Germany.

My parents and my youngest brother Dietmar gave Elaine an enthusiastic welcome which could only be kept in check by the unavoidable linguistic barriers. Brother Dietmar's school English and my mother's dexterous use of a dictionary all helped to overcome the initial hesitancy.

Seeing how readily and enthusiastically Elaine was establishing a rapport not only with my family, but also with friends and acquaintances, I found it easier by the hour to convince myself that I should grasp the opportunity to propose to her here and now. Should I telephone her mother first and go through the formality of seeking her official consent?

Somehow I had felt for some time now that Elaine's mother had made up her mind that even with my foreign background I could be an acceptable suitor and partner for her daughter. Her own lifestyle was outgoing, embracing people of many different backgrounds, and being a successful business woman had given her the additional capacity of confronting problems in a balanced and cool-headed manner. Within these character attributes, however, came also the expectancy of complete loyalty from people nearest to her and above all from her daughter Elaine.

Ever since I first set foot in Elaine's home it had been obvious how strong a bond existed between mother and daughter and, as future events demonstrated, Elaine's submission to her mother's dominant role was in the end the decisive factor that led to a decisive change in my own life.

And so it finally happened. Sheltered from the noise of those outside crowds with their wooden rattles, drums and other noise-making devices, and enjoying what came nearest to a traditional English afternoon tea in the comfortable surrounds of the Colombi Hotel, I asked Elaine to become my wife. What had I done? I did not go down on my knee. And no ring!

Well, at least you got it off your chest and I presume the young lady asked for time to think about it.

Yes, that was really the response I had expected, but to my astonishment and delight Elaine responded with an enthusiastic "Yes!", adding however that we should both give ourselves some time before tying the proverbial knot. Did this indicate that she would first of all like to acquaint herself more thoroughly with life in Germany? Was this her first attempt to escape her mother's influence? Whatever the reason, at this precise moment I wanted to savour her spontaneous acceptance and to crown it all I insisted that we pay an immediate visit to the jewellers next to the hotel. The shop assistant, after discretely trying to establish a bearable price spectrum, presented a large range of engagement rings with different stones and decorative markings. His ability to offer his goods in near perfect English certainly helped Elaine to come to a much quicker decision than I had expected.

Our news met with an enthusiastic response from my own parents and to my relief also from Elaine's mother. Amongst the well wishes for our joint future, however, there was a conspicuous absence of the expected questions about how and where we were planning to set up home, and where and when we were to get married. In a truly diplomatic fashion, these matters were pushed into the long grass, which suited us well as we would not have known how to answer such questions anyway.

With the whole town engulfed in a state of noisy merriment, and people, despite the low temperatures, walking about in flimsy and often grotesque-looking costumes, all was set for the grand Rosenmontag parade. And what did Elaine produce out of her suspiciously large suitcase? A complete costume of a poodle dog. Was she out to steal the show? All I could muster was a rather shabby-looking tweed jacket with matching flat cap, a pair of trousers that had seen better days and a hideous large moustache held on with an uncomfortable clip up my nostrils.

The pavements were filled with cheering crowds as the parade, starting at the Karlsplatz, made its way down the Kaiserstrasse. At the halfway stage, Elaine suddenly reminded me that she still had not made the daily telephone call on which her mother had insisted before she had given her approval for this solo trip to Freiburg. The nearest telephone was at the main post office where overseas calls still had to be booked via a switchboard operator. The young switchboard lady went out of her way to compliment Elaine on her unusual costume, which, to my growing irritation and all being said in German, resulted in us spending nearly an hour of precious Rosenmontag time in a post office. I had felt very tempted to ask Elaine to give this call a miss on this special day, but having by now become familiar with the unquestioning obedience demanded by her mother I knew that there would be no other event important enough to allow any form of disobedience.

The moment of Elaine's return came all too soon, but when at our parting at Basel Airport Elaine told me that her mother had already suggested to spend their next holiday in Freiburg my hopes were given a real uplift. Was there after all the prospect of a joint future in Germany? With promises of regular contact by mail and telephone, we finally savoured our last embrace and I waved her off through the departure door.

Back in Freiburg, I was quickly reabsorbed into the lively atmosphere of a university town and above all my new junior management function made sure I had not too much time to ponder excessively about my longer-term future with Elaine. With snow conditions at the Feldberg still excellent, some weekend skiing rekindled my appreciation of this sport.

To my delight Elaine turned out to be a very regular and prolific letter writer, with a style of writing that was very descriptive. It was obvious that she and her friend, Sylvia, were not short of invitations to Makerston House parties and Elaine's descriptions of old and new Makerston House residents and their personal stories were so vivid that I almost felt like I was there as a participant. Unfortunately, I could not match this accomplished level of reporting, since, although mastering now the spoken English without major problems, my ability to express myself in written form was still far from perfect.

It must have been the middle of the year when I received a letter from Elaine's mother informing me that her daughter had to be hospitalised with a serious eye problem, but that she was on the road to recovery, cheered on by several of the Makerstonians who had visited her at the hospital. The letter contained also the first concrete proposal for a visit to Freiburg in the hope that I can equally arrange an August holiday for myself.

Was this now Elaine's mother's scouting trip to find out more about what life in Germany was like and also to explore more as to how I could possibly ensure for her daughter the lifestyle she presently enjoys? Or, having thought more about our recent engagement and the geographical implications, was the purpose of this visit to point out face to face all the impracticalities and problems which lay ahead? I feared the latter might be the case. Even my parents, after their initial enthusiastic response to our announcement, let slip the odd comment seeking to find out more as to how Elaine and I had envisaged a future together.

With Elaine out of hospital, our correspondence restarted with undiminished vigour, untroubled by any of the doubts which may have started to affect our elders.

My thoughts turned now to setting the scene for a memorable holiday for Elaine and her mother as August was approaching with relentless speed. Judging by what I had heard in the past about their holidays in Austria and Switzerland, I booked accommodation in a good hotel near the Colombi Park and I mapped out several excursions by car to some of the tourist top spots of the upper Rhine region, including a visit to Lake Constance and the island of Mainau. Above all, however, I wanted them to see more of Freiburg itself and its picturesque surroundings, including the quaint villages of the nearby Kaiserstuhl, renowned for their production of excellent wines. And then, of course, I could not leave out a train journey up the awe-inspiring Hoellental to Lake Tittisee, a tourist attraction which seemed to be popular with visitors from many foreign countries. And in all this I included also a brief visit to Munich, the metropolis I had become so fond of and which I was sure would equally entrance my visitors. All in all, I thought that I had devised a programme which would portray my country in a very positive picture and that with the welcoming attitude of my own family and also my circle of friends, life in this environment would become a palatable proposition.

And so the crucial day finally arrived. Two elegantly

dressed ladies appeared at the exit gate at Basel Airport and the amount of baggage on their trolley sent out a clear message that they had come well prepared for any sartorial demands during their holiday.

To my relief, the hotel arrangement got Elaine's mother full approval, as did my outline description of the plans for the days ahead. The warm welcome by my own parents and Freiburg, in full bloom and bustling with tourists, provided a perfect start for an interesting holiday. I, of course, wanted it to be more than a holiday. Could I make them feel at home here?

The next few days made me realise that being a tourist guide can be quite a demanding job. Our two-day visit to Munich was a real personal treat as it brought back memories of the happy days I had spent there in the past and enabled me to meet up again with my old friend Walter. An unexpected indisposition of Elaine and a brief but successful visit to the hospital added to the excitement of this trip.

After visiting villages around the Kaiserstuhl, the shores of Lake Constance and the picturesque island of Mainau and also the obligatory train journey to Tittisee, it came finally as a real relief just to explore the beauty spots of Freiburg itself. And there was very little to surpass an afternoon at the Dattler Café, high above the town, indulging in an elegantly served coffee with a mouth-watering piece of cake, whilst enjoying a full view of the town below with the majestic minster as its centre point.

When finally the day of departure arrived, I could not suppress my feeling that my efforts to obtain at least an indication from Elaine that a joint future in Germany might be a possibility, had failed. She had been received with warmth and friendliness by everyone she had met, she clearly liked Freiburg and the surrounding countryside, the meals seemed to have been to her liking and she had even learnt not to rush across the road when the traffic lights clearly indicated to pedestrians not to cross. Above all her feelings for me seemed to be as strong as ever. And yet, our joint future was no more than a mirage in the hot desert sand.

After yet another emotional farewell at the Basel Airport we comforted each other with the promise of a reunion in Scotland for Christmas and in the meantime to share each other's life through regular correspondence.

Thankfully my work in the office became increasingly demanding which helped to make the Christmas season approach more quickly. My parents, who had clearly become very fond of Elaine, were very understanding that once again I would not be around for the festive days and with brother Lothar also away in South Africa our little brother Dietmar was left to deputise for his two absent brothers.

Flying between Basel and Glasgow's Renfrew Airport began to feel like a routine event, not so different from what nowadays would be described as long-distance commuting.

It became yet another action-packed Christmas with visits to members of the wider family and close friends, including another memorable and enjoyable visit to the MacKellar family in Greenock. It was on a return journey from one of these visits that Elaine's mother let the cat out of the bag by implying how nice it would be if the Company gave me a job in Glasgow or even somewhere else in the UK.

It strikes me that whilst you are doing your utmost to present Germany as a palatable location for your joint future with Elaine, mother and daughter are obviously pursuing a decidedly different agenda.

Elaine's non-committal reaction after the summer holiday in Freiburg had already made me start to think along those lines myself, but with our relationship remaining as close as ever – in fact growing in spite of our infrequent encounters – I was not giving up hope yet.

Chapter 11

It must have been late February when another member of my department in Freiburg was allocated to me to act as my full-time assistant. It was only two to three weeks later that the reason for this became obvious. I was informed that Glasgow Head Office had decided to continue with my training programme, which involved firstly a product evaluation study in the USA and then I was to proceed to Australia for a period still to be defined. Work permits and visas soon filled several pages of my passport and above all, before setting out on this new adventure, I was to spend two weeks at the Glasgow offices and be domiciled once again in Makerston House.

It took quite some time for all this to sink in. The tingling sensation of adventure began to grip me again, but without the element of fear which was my regular companion when in my younger days I ventured across the Iron Curtain.

My parents were delighted to see me being offered such an exciting opportunity to visit such far-flung places, and Elaine seemed to be thrilled to see me back in Scotland so soon after the Christmas break. I think the news might have made them think that my professional future might not lie in Germany after all and that the Company had other plans for me.

With me now becoming an international traveller, my

parents thought that I needed to travel with a more stylish suitcase. One evening, after my return from the office, a very smart-looking leather case awaited me in our lounge, already partially filled with a range of new shirts, underwear and a pair of pyjamas. In the past I had always strongly objected to my mother doing the packing for me, but this was a farewell of a different kind and I have to admit, I had a slight tremor in my voice when I thanked my parents for their generous farewell gift.

On 14th April 1960, I landed once again at Glasgow's Renfrew Airport and after a taxi ride through Paisley past my old training ground, Anchor Mill, I reached Makerston House where Mrs Jamieson greeted me like a long-lost son. It really felt like my second home.

It was all like a throwback to the earlier days of our courtship, except that our past joint lunch breaks in the coffee houses of Sauchiehall were no longer possible since her employer had moved their offices to their large industrial complex at Ardeer on the Ayrshire coast. The residents at Makerston House were a completely new generation and Mrs Jamieson went to great lengths to tell me of the whereabouts of my earlier contemporaries, who, unlike myself, had had no prior connection with one of the Company's many subsidiaries and who found themselves being sent off to different countries round the globe.

In the Glasgow offices however, little seemed to have changed and I was received again with the same cordiality and friendliness as when I first set foot in there two years ago. When I jokingly apologised for not turning up properly attired with the customary bowler hat because my new suitcase was too small for it, the personnel manager informed me with a stern face that this was no longer a cause for instant dismissal on top of which he added that wearing this symbol of British male respectability would most likely only lead to sniggering comments in the places I was about to visit. After vetting my passport to ensure that I had all the necessary permits for entering the USA and Australia, I was given my flight ticket to New York which, to my surprise, informed me that on this occasion I would depart from Prestwick Airport. At New York Idlewild Airport, a member of the local Coats office would meet me and would take me to a pre-booked accommodation near the Company office. The onward ticket to Australia would be provided by the New York office. The arrangements once again bore all the hallmarks of an efficient organisation and it really made me feel proud to be part of it all.

And all too soon the final day arrived. The farewell party at Makerston House was quite subdued compared with the decidedly boisterous events with my earlier contemporaries. Thankfully it was an early evening departure from Prestwick which enabled Elaine and her mother to drive me to the airport. Farewells at airports and railway stations very often turn into tumultuous displays of sentimentality with an endless repetition of good wishes and reassurances to keep in touch. I was glad that our goodbye followed that pattern in a more modest mode. Whilst deploring having to part with Elaine, once again the thought of the adventure ahead seemed to make the parting much easier.

After a comfortable overnight flight, I finally arrived in New York on Thursday 28th April 1960.After passing through immigration control without any problem, and having retrieved my suitcase, I soon spotted a gentleman holding up a piece of paper with my name on it. It all seemed so easy.

I had seen many pictures of the New York skyline before, but here I was now being driven through the streets with towering giants on either side.

"You are booked into a place in Lexington Avenue," my driver explained, "and here is a letter and a map as you are expected in the office tomorrow morning."

When I produced my German passport to the receptionist I was wondering if the Americans would show any lingering animosity to anything German, but my fears were unfounded. I quickly gained the impression that the Americans looked upon the last war as a painful and unwanted involvement in a global conflict and once drawn into it they had to play their part with the same ferocity and determination as their European and Far Eastern foes. Yet I also gained the impression during my encounters with individuals during the next few days that several of them felt that the events at Dresden and Hiroshima and Nagasaki had somewhat muddied the heroic image of their victory, and they expressed their relief for not having had to endure the traumas of bombing raids and fire storms in their own home land, except for one visible scar which I had already planned to see on my onward journey.

My reception in the office the next morning was even

more friendly and spontaneous than my very first day at the Head Office in Glasgow. I was treated more like a curiosity and everybody was much more forthcoming with questions and observations than our more reserved Head Office colleagues in Scotland. However, the speed at which people spoke, the choice of words and the general intonation made me feel a little insecure for a day or two.

My guide and mentor turned out to be a charming gentleman of second-generation Irish immigrants. He not only briefed me on the product study I was to carry out, but also offered me a place at his family house in New Jersey from the beginning of the following week. A wonderful and generous show of hospitality. It would give me a chance to see how Americans lived and with this only starting on Monday I would have the weekend all to myself to explore some of the famous landmarks of New York. After all, would I ever come back here again? I surely could not send any postcards back home to my parents and Elaine without stating that I had been up to the top of the Empire State Building! For reasons I cannot remember, I had also put the Waldorf Astoria Hotel on my must-see list. On Sunday, properly attired I walked past the doorman into the magnificent foyer and treated myself to afternoon tea. After a relaxing hour of trying to work out the different languages spoken by guests passing my table, I left with my trophy —a napkin with the Waldorf Astoria imprint as evidence of my visit to this famous establishment. To this was added the ticket for my visit to the top deck of the Empire State Building. From then onwards it was work.

On Monday morning, having checked out from my Lexington Avenue residence, I treated myself to one of those yellow taxis, as I did not feel like walking with my heavy suitcase to the Company offices.

What did my mentor have in store for me? For the next three days I became an assistant jobber, visiting department stores and smaller retailers where our Company representative not only took orders for Coats' products for later delivery, but where he also restocked metal display carousels with bobbins of sewing thread individually wrapped up in transparent blister packs. It was certainly a novel idea of selling our products and I felt sure that this type of marketing and product presentation would also appeal to our urban European customers. I was not sure however if all those kindly lady owners of haberdashery shops in those remote villages in Scotland would readily approve of such a novelty presentation which after all had to be paid for.

The days flew by only too quickly. In fact, the whole tempo of life was so much faster and also on a much grander scale. The people themselves appeared to be taller and more heavily built, probably resulting from the large servings in restaurants and in their own homes as I had already noticed when sharing meals with my host family. Their motorcars looked decidedly oversized and I must admit less elegant than European vehicles, but there was a sense of vibrancy which was almost infectious.

The relationship between our Company representative and his customers was cordial, but lacked the intimacy which I had witnessed in Scotland and even Germany. The pressure of time left no room for indulging in long spells of questioning as to where I came from and why I was spending time in New York. Offerings of tea and scones were now merely a treasured memory from my earlier days of my journey into the unknown.

And yet there was another side to life in this New World. Staying with my mentor in his family home in New Jersey I could not have asked for a more friendly and relaxed family environment. The red hair of my mentor's two daughters left no doubt about their Celtic ancestry and their inquisitiveness revealed lively and searching minds. Life in this family home stood in stark contrast to the relentless and competitive nature of the business world outside.

Midweek after having completed another day as an assistant jobber, the office manager asked me to see him to discuss my onward travel to Australia.

"As you are a newcomer to our country," he said, "we felt that you should not just take away the impressions of this city but also have a brief look around in our other well-known metropolis on the West Coast – San Francisco."

I could hardly believe what I had just heard.

"Here is your ticket to San Francisco on Friday morning," he added, "and a room reservation at the Sun Rise Hotel close to the airport. This second ticket here will then transport you on Sunday in the direction of Australia, via our beautiful and also tragic islands of Hawaii. Since civil aircraft tend to have an extra-long refuelling stop over at Honolulu before setting off on their long trans-pacific flight to Australia, you may have an opportunity to see some part

167

of this island, which as you probably know was the scene of a horrific aggression in 1941 and which brought our country into the global conflict of World War Two.

"Mr Bradley, your host, has kindly agreed to take you directly from his home to the airport on Friday. If you finish your report on the marketing possibilities in Europe for blister pack presentations before your departure you can give it to your host. We shall forward it to Glasgow and send you a copy at the office in Sydney."

After all this, my head was in a complete spin. Everything was organised with so much care and foresight and I was almost finding myself short of the right words to express my thanks for what my American colleagues had done for me.

It sounds to me you are just about to enter another phase on your journey into the unknown. To get there, however, seems to have become a real joyride compared with the perils of your travels as a young boy in those early post-war years.

Yes, you are right, Joseph. Compared with what one can now easily be described as reckless travelling in my teenage years, this now lacked all the perils and yet it retained the features of a challenging adventure and I loved every moment of it.

The long flight to San Francisco made me aware of the huge dimensions of this country. Having secured a window seat and with the sky being almost cloudless, I gazed at the ever-changing landscape below me. It was almost like a kaleidoscope with towns, large lakes, forests and rugged mountains appearing in intermittent succession. When the in-flight meal was served the well-dressed gentleman sitting next to me started to engage me in a conversation which soon developed into him making a series of suggestions as what to do and what to see in San Francisco. When I told him that it was only a short stop-over for me as I was really on my way to Australia, he suggested that a visit to the San Francisco Bay should be top of my list to see not only a masterpiece of American engineering, the Golden Gate Bridge, but also the small rocky island of Alcatraz with its infamous prison for America's most troublesome criminals.

"And if you have some time to spare," he added, "do not miss the opportunity to visit our famous Chinatown which, although on our shores, transports you completely into the ethos, traditions and even smells of Chinese culture. It is a great tourist attraction and with China itself in such a turmoil it is the best substitute for a visit to that country you will ever get."

As to be expected, he could not suppress his own curiosity about my reason for being on this flight en route to Australia and when I let slip that my own origin was German he explained that his own forebearers had come from Italy and first settled in New York, but then decided to move to California because the climate there was more akin to that of their homeland.

During the next day, following the suggestions of my fellow traveller, I started to explore this fascinating city. Unlike New York, this was a very hilly place and quaint-looking tram cars seemed to be the main means of transport paying remarkable disregard for the often steep gradients of the city's roads. There was a decidedly different feel to this city compared with New York. The architecture looked different and the sky scrapers did not have that almost menacing effect which on several occasions I had felt in New York. It really was a wonderful gesture of my Coats' colleagues in New York to let me have this experience. My fellow traveller on the plane had not exaggerated when he put a visit to the shoreline of the San Francisco Bay at the top of my must-see list. It was already late in the afternoon and the rays of the sun seemed to give the majestic bridge a subtle golden glow which may well have led its original builders to call it the Golden Gate Bridge.

And then, about two kilometres out in the middle of the Bay, there was America's most-feared prison, Alcatraz. A young boy standing next to me tried to show off his knowledge of this forbidding place by informing me that way back, before the war, America's most notorious gangster Al Capone was incarcerated there for over 10 years. Today, he added, the penitentiary houses only a few prisoners and their treatment is said to be much more humane than in the past. I thanked him for his short history lesson and headed back into the city for a brief foray into the highly recommended Chinatown. Maybe it was a culture shock, but somehow I did not feel comfortable exploring the mysteries of the East amongst this clearly booming and vibrant Chinese community on the American continent. So I soon headed back to my hotel enjoying a few more rides on those unique tram cars

The take-off in the morning provided another magnificent view of the Golden Gate Bridge, but from then on it was nearly six hours of nothing but the Pacific Ocean below me. The traveller next to me, a middle-aged lady, was deeply absorbed in numerous fashion magazines and from her general composure one could tell she was not interested in small talk with her fellow traveller. That suited me quite well as I had seriously fallen behind with my letter writing to Elaine and I also finished off a few San Francisco postcards to my parents and friends in Freiburg and Munich, for posting at my last USA stopover in Hawaii.

The name itself had reawakened memories of the evening way back in 1958 when I took Elaine to the cinema in Paisley to watch the just-released film sensation *South Pacific*. With only three hours to spare before my next take-off, would there be a chance to savour some of the romantic atmosphere of this place myself? Always having had a keen interest in the historical events that eventually led to the outbreak of World War Two and having read that the airport in Honolulu was not very far from the naval base of Pearl Harbour, it had been my intention to use my stopover time for a visit to what was the only place in the USA that had ever experienced the traumas of ferocious aerial bombing.

After finally arriving at Honolulu Airport, I was ushered into a transit lounge where I was informed that after depositing my German passport and my onward flight ticket with the uniformed official at the reception desk, I could leave the airport building and visit places of interest on the island, but that I would have to be back for embarkation within three hours. When I expressed to the official my interest in visiting the Pearl Harbour site he indicated that apart from the hull of the sunken battleship *Arizona* protruding from the harbour water, there were no visible reminders of that infamous event in 1941.

"After all," he added, "all that happened nearly 20 years ago. You would learn more about our island by going down to the beach, and this being a Sunday, you can feast your eyes on a fantastic gathering of our local beach beauties."

I did not need more persuading and when I finally settled down in the shade of a large palm tree on the edge of the beach my only regret was that I had no bathing trunks to join those joyful crowds on the beach and in the water. And as the airport official had already indicated, there was no shortage of Hawaiian beauties in colourful skimpy swimwear.

Listening to you, I take it that this visit to the beach fulfilled some of the romantic expectations you had from seeing that famous film so many years ago, and no doubt it was more scintillating than looking at the remains of a sunken battleship.

Absolutely right, Joseph. After all, in the past I had seen already more than enough of the sufferings and destruction meted out on all sides during the last war and visiting yet another war memorial on this beautiful island would merely have satisfied my curiosity, but prevented me from experiencing this peaceful and joyful scene on this glorious beach.

Back at the airport, when collecting my passport and my flight ticket, I thanked that friendly official for his good advice which allowed me to leave this romantic island with very pleasant memories, so different from the reminders of the last war, which I had originally planned to visit.

The next stopover was Suva in Fiji. Once again, refuelling and servicing of the aircraft provided a long enough break for the passengers to venture outside the airport building. The row of stalls outside the building was a clear indication that these stopovers were a regular source of income for the stallholders and most of my fellow travellers did not take long to wander along these stalls in search of a typical Fijian souvenir. On one of the stalls my eyes were caught by a delicate necklace made from local shells. My remaining few US dollars were just enough to clinch the deal, although the trader who spoke fluent English assured me that payment in Australian pounds would have been equally acceptable. Not having acquired any souvenirs for Elaine in the USA, this was really my last opportunity to acquire a gift for her before reaching the end of a journey which had opened up such an exciting new world for me.

After another flight of over four hours, we were finally rewarded with a splendid view of the Sydney Harbour Bridge before touching down at the city's airport. Would my reception be similar to my arrival in New York?

When I presented my passport to the immigration official I remember him flicking through it page by page until ending up with the work permit for Australia, issued by their Embassy in far-away Cologne.

"I see it is valid for one year," he said, "but the initial entry permit will only be for six months and then you need to reapply for the remaining six months. Who knows, you might even decide to stay a lot longer or decide to make this your new home."

A rather unusual welcome, I thought, and I was beginning to wonder what the next reception would be like in the arrivals hall.

A very casually dressed man standing close to the exit door held up a board with my name on it. Grabbing my suitcase and confining his conversational skills to a mere "Welcome to Australia" he led me to the taxi rank outside the building where one of the vehicles turned out to be his. Once there he handed me a large envelope, which he had been told to give to me on my arrival. The whole procedure turned out to be identical to my arrival at Idlewild Airport in New York, except that the driver was decidedly less talkative and inquisitive and what he spoke revealed yet another deviation from the Queen's English.

It soon became obvious that all things from buildings to motor cars were on a more modest scale compared with New York or San Francisco. No intimidating skyscrapers but rows of attractive one and two storey houses. With traffic on the left again and street names of English towns and landmarks flashing past me, it quickly filled me with a pleasant feeling of familiarity.

When we finally stopped, I found myself facing a rather modest-looking building surrounded by shrubs and trees and a small sign with the name Fairclough Hotel. A cheerful middle-aged lady dealt very swiftly with the check-in formalities and then led me to my room on the ground floor.

"I have a garden room for you," she said. "You must keep the backdoor closed to stop snakes and spiders from entering."

That was certainly a novel piece of advice when staying in a hotel room.

The room itself was rather dark and small and both the wardrobe and table and chair had seen better days. Compared with accommodation I had become accustomed to over the last few years, this fell well below those standards. However, here I was and I had to face up to it. Was this going to be my abode for my whole stay in Australia?

When I finally opened the envelope the driver had given to me at the airport it contained not only a cheerful and welcoming letter from the local office manager plus instructions on how to reach the Coats offices, but also a note saying that my present accommodation was for only one week after which I will transfer to a new address at Ormond Hall in New South Head Road in the suburb of Vaucluse. It all sounded reassuring and comforting and once again demonstrated the caring behaviour of the Company which by now I had almost taken for granted.

Unlike the modern offices in New York, the Sydney offices in Druitt Street, close to the harbour area, looked more like a large warehouse, more akin to the Distribution Centre at the Ferguslie Mill in Paisley.

The office manager took it upon himself to introduce me personally to each member of staff who all appeared rather young and more casually dressed then I had seen in other Company offices. There was also a local management trainee, called Keith, who became a good friend and guide in the months ahead.

My work schedule was laid out in considerable detail and covered all the administrative functions within the local organisation.

"Some of our customers are reluctant to part with the money they owe us," the manager added, "and you might like to hone your skills of persuasion or compulsion by working in that department for the first two weeks."

Not exactly the easiest of starts, I thought to myself.

The whole atmosphere in the office was pleasantly informal, almost bordering on occasional irreverence to senior staff.

When I was invited to join my new colleagues for a lunch break at a nearby bar I was also offered a glass of their local beer. It felt like gulping down the still liquid refreshment from a deep freezer.

With Keith's guidance I soon became familiar with the local layout and also the social and cultural events in this bustling city. After only a few days he had enrolled me as a member of an international club for young people at a location with the familiar name of

Kings Cross. The club was like a magnet, pulling in young newcomers to Sydney, many of whom were recent immigrants from Europe.

When I told Keith that my stay in a hotel would only be temporary and that the Company had rented a small apartment for me in Vaucluse he congratulated me but could not refrain from adding that trainees from overseas were clearly provided with superior accommodation compared with local trainees like himself.

And superior it was. The house was set in beautiful gardens. The interior was divided into four individual apartments and I was awaited by a well-dressed gentleman who introduced himself as the representative of the letting agency to provide me with the key to an upper floor apartment and a card with the addresses of nearby shops and a laundrette. It all felt very homely and, being at the rear of the building, I had an unobstructed view of the sea over the tops of some lower lying houses and rows of trees. As I found out later, it was only a short walk to a small sandy beach.

The comradeship which seemed to characterise this organisation from top to bottom made the working weeks fly past very quickly. On top of this, many of the tasks were not unfamiliar to me as I had performed them at some stage in my earlier training both in Germany and the UK.

Did you ever ask yourself, why did the Company send you to the other side of the world for more training?

Good question, Joseph, and I am afraid I have no real answer. Was it a sign of being prepared for international duties as a member of the parent company in Glasgow, rather than return to Germany? Events that followed only eight months later seemed to point in that direction, but at this point I did not really care about the purpose of my secondment to Australia because with every passing week I grew fonder of life in a country which was so free of the shackles of social barriers, so prevalent in many of the countries of Europe. What had the immigration official said to me at the airport? 'Maybe you will decide to make this your new home.' An interesting thought, but having failed so far to persuade Elaine to even committing herself to a future in Germany I did not think that an even more remote country would meet with her – or more precisely her mother's – approval. Also with Elaine's comportment and sometimes excessive observance of social niceties, I doubted if this outpost of the British Empire would lure her away from her set ways in her traditional Scottish home.

Chapter 12

To my surprise my new colleagues, and also my new acquaintances at the International Club, showed an unexpected disinterest in my own background, unlike the ever-present curiosity displayed by people in Scotland, England or by staff in the New York office. Somehow Europe with its past and present problems took second place to often animated discussions about their own outdoor life, horse racing, fishing, even gold panning in the nearby mountains, cricket and rugby and the occasional flare-up in relations between organised labour organisations and employers. It all sounded so much simpler and uncomplicated and although it may have lacked the sophistication of society in their mother country, the simplicity and earthiness evident in most aspects of daily life here was most refreshing and appealed to me very much.

One day I was asked to join one of our sales representatives on a three-day trip into the Sydney hinterland beyond the Blue Mountain range, to visit not only wholesale and retail customers but also some outlying farms that had traditionally received an annual visit by the Coats representative to supply them with their threads and needles for the year ahead.

The Australian-made Holden car was clearly designed to withstand not only the rigours of steep roads through the picturesque Blue Mountain range, but also the rugged terrain en route to some remote farmsteads. It was my first encounter with kangaroos, often crossing the track in great leaps right in front of our car.

Our first stop was in a town called Katoomba, which I was told had featured quite predominantly in the Australian goldrush. In fact, at weekends the area continued to attract enterprising visitors from Sydney to try their luck with their panning bowls in the numerous mountain streams.

When visiting our first customer, one immediately realised the difference to the establishments in Europe. Here the atmosphere of the frontier country was still evident. The shops had to cater for all the needs of their customers. It was therefore not unusual for our products to be displayed next to hand tools, ranges of crockery and kitchen utensils and personal hygiene products.

I enjoyed every minute of this trip. The reception we received from our customers was decidedly more boisterous than what I remembered from my visits to those inquisitive lady owners of haberdashery shops in the Scottish Highlands. Now, however, my presence was quickly explained with the laconic remark, "He is here to learn the trade." That rarely led to further questions.

Our next stop was in Bathurst, with its impressive railway station and other elegant buildings and parks, not unlike a Scottish market town. Some of the shops we visited were more focused on specific lines of merchandise, but the frontier spirit still prevailed.

A visit to two outlying sheep farms concluded this much-cherished trip into the Australian outback. Our representative was received like a long-lost friend by the farmers' families and having been able to meet all their requirements from the stock carried in the back of our Holden car we were invited to join them for refreshments before setting out on our long journey back to Sydney. Back at the office, when thanking the manager for giving me the opportunity for such a unique experience, another surprise was in store for me.

"On your next trip," he said, "you will not have any kangaroos galloping across your path, but we have arranged for you to spend a few days with our colleagues at the Melbourne office and for this journey you can travel by a comfortable train."

What other exciting surprises had they lined up for me?

It really looks to me that Australia had received you with open arms. All you need now is to fall for the charms of a local beauty and Australia might indeed become your future.

It is strange, you should mention this at this moment. The flow of correspondence between Elaine and myself continued unabated and with undiminished passion and expressions of affection. It immunised me to the flirtatious overtures by several female members of the International Club. When I told them that I was only on a temporary secondment to Australia their interest generally faded quite quickly as they were clearly looking for partners with a long-term future in this country. However, I did not escape the clutches of the female gender completely.

One evening on the tram back to Vaucluse I happened to sit next to a middle-aged lady, one of those outgoing characters who love to engage people in conversation whenever an opportunity arises. She quickly extracted from me my German background and expressed her wish to learn more about my past. By the time she left the tram at Rose Bay we had agreed to meet again at her house the coming weekend.

This chance encounter turned into a memorable friendship for the rest of my stay in Australia. Her name was Norma Berman. Working for a Sydney radio station her interest in national and international events always resulted in lively discussions with groups of people from her large social circle. My fellow trainee, Keith, soon joined our gatherings and was equally enthralled by this lady, who having been widowed a few years earlier had not lost her zest for life as an inspiring hostess but also as a mother and grandmother to her family based in Adelaide.

The train journey to Melbourne provided me with yet another experience. I remembered the reports from the early war years when, amongst announcing the successes of the German army on the eastern front, considerable tribute was paid to the engineers who enabled the German rolling stock to function on the much wider rail tracks in Russia. I had not expected to find a divergence of rail tracks within the boundaries of one nation like Australia. But here I was, setting off early in the morning for my long journey south. After numerous stops en route, we finally reached a town called Albury where we had to leave our coaches and join another train on the other side of a very wide platform. We had reached the state of Victoria where the railway system used a wider track gauge than the neighbouring state of New South Wales. Certainly a novel experience, but I heard years later that in 1962 this anomaly was finally resolved with the adoption of the standard European gauge for most of the country.

Melbourne turned out to be a more impressive city than I had expected. Old colonial-type buildings, some of them built with what looked like bluish-tinged stone, sided with imposing modern office blocks and wherever one looked green-beige coloured tram cars seemed to be trundling along in all directions. People looked well dressed, with many gentlemen in dark business suits. It reminded me of my days at Glasgow Head Office, except that here the bowler hat was replaced by sporty looking trilby hats.

The reception in the office was once again most welcoming, with several members of staff only too anxious to tell me more about their city. In fact, the manager suggested that before delving into the business side of my visit, a member of staff would collect me the following morning from my hotel to give me a guided tour of the city. With a jocular undertone, he added that after all Melbourne is the cultural capital of Australia.

A young male office clerk duly turned up the following morning.

"I hope you like riding by tram cars," he said, "because that is our mode of transport for the day."

I had already been truly impressed by the tram network

in Sydney, but what I experienced here exceeded everything I had previously come across, even in Europe. At one point my guide drew my attention to a tall building which he said was one of the latest additions to the Melbourne skyline. It was called the ICI Building and housed the offices of a large UK industrial conglomerate. Little did I know at this stage what role this company would play one day in my own future. Their offices in Sauchiehall Street in Glasgow looked decidedly more modest.

The three days allotted to this visit passed by only too quickly. Our customers here in Melbourne seemed to be more diverse in trades and industry than in Sydney. A large Chinese community represented an interesting, albeit fiercely competitive business opportunity. Also, the widespread presence of customers with a central European background fuelled a good demand for embroidery products. Even my own countrymen must have settled here in larger numbers and chose Heidelberg as the name for their new home here on the outskirts of Melbourne. It was a fascinating three days, with yet another insight into the world down under.

In my comfortable seat on the train back to Sydney, my thoughts began to wander back to Scotland, to Elaine, my own family and friends in Freiburg and Munich. Would my present enthusiasm for the Australian way of life eventually cool off and leave me yearning again for Europe, the old world which after all was on the brink of re-establishing itself again as a cultural trendsetter for the whole globe? Would the Coats Company be sympathetic to any request to become a permanent member of staff of their Australian organisation?

By the time the train reached Sydney, these self-critical questions left me in a true state of confusion, but thankfully not for long.

Back at my Vaucluse apartment, three letters were waiting for me. There is often a moment of apprehension before opening letters and I certainly felt it on this occasion, with one letter being from Elaine, the second one from her mother and the last one from my own mother. Have they all decided that our engagement should be called off?

After having read the letters, I felt almost ashamed of myself for ever having harboured such thoughts. In fact, the warmth and intimacy of all three letters quickly removed any doubts as to where I belong. I found myself at peace with myself again.

Back at the office I was told to take on the role of stock controller and purchasing clerk as a stand-in for staff going on their annual leave. Keith excelled himself in making sure that at weekends I shared the Australian's love for the outdoor life with river cruises, repeated visits to Manly Beach and even some horse riding.

One day when leaving Circular Quay for Manly we witnessed the take-off of a huge flying boat, skimming for a very long distance over the harbour waters before finally lifting off into the air.

"It is a regular service to Lord Howe Island," Keith explained, "and with no land-based airstrip there, flying boats are the only solution."

The harbour was indeed a hub of constant activity and

with its imposing bridge, a sight to behold.

It must have been the following week when back at the harbour we watched the arrival of a large liner from Genoa. The quayside was packed with people, gesticulating excitedly to the passengers, lining the portside railing of the ship. The gangway had not yet been lowered when suddenly one young man started to use one of the thick mooring ropes to clamber up to the ship's deck.

"These are all Italian immigrants," Keith explained, "but amongst them will also be a large number of young unattached *signoras* who will be eagerly awaited by the sizeable community of resident Italian bachelors. That fellow climbing up the rope clearly wants to make sure his act of bravado secures him a sure place in the hearts of some of those young ladies."

Judging by the cheering from the ship's railing, Keith's description may well have been right.

I could hardly believe that over five months had passed since my arrival. With such a busy and exiting lifestyle, I had completely forgotten to seek the official extension to my residence and work permit, initially valid for only six months. Thankfully, a letter arrived at the office reminding me of the need to renew my permits and early September I received an official extension until May 1961.

I seem to remember that you were not given a clear indication as to the length of this extra training period. Did you think that you might stay in Australia until the end of your permit?

It had crossed my mind several times as to why until now I had not been given any further information about my eventual return to Europe. Had the local manager received further details but was not passing them on to me? In the end, I approached him and he admitted that he had indeed received a letter from Head Office. It stipulated that I should report back to Glasgow before Christmas, but that the precise day of departure from Australia was left to his discretion. He added that the letter contained the suggestion that since I had not taken any annual leave, the Sydney office might time my departure in such a way as to catch one of the liners sailing back to the UK. Here I was expecting to fly back to my previous job in Freiburg when in fact there was now the exciting prospect of sailing westwards, concluding a complete round-the-world-trip. It was only a month ago that I had noticed the liner *Orsova* in Sydney Harbour and the thought of spending 30 days on such a ship was really too much to hope for.

"However, before we organise your return," he continued, "I have marked you down for the first three weeks of October to be the acting manager of our Brisbane branch office. The local manager wants to take an extended annual holiday to visit friends and family in his native Scotland. We have a small but competent team there and I am sure this will be a new and satisfying experience during your time with us."

On my way home to Vaucluse I was completely oblivious to the overcrowded tram car, as my mind was trying to digest what I had been told earlier on. A voyage back to the UK, no word about returning to Freiburg. Christmas with

Elaine? What was going on?

The next day, on my way to the office I stopped at a jeweller's shop to which I had never paid much attention in the past. I had heard that Australia prides itself on their high-quality opals. Although I had already purchased a toy koala bear, I was sure that an extra little gem from here would go down very well as a Christmas present. The shopowner explained to me the quality differences and colour combinations and we soon agreed on a small stone which he said could be set in any casing by a qualified goldsmith. It felt like another high point in an eventful week.

In the past, the Queensland administration had clearly shown more forward vision by adopting the same rail gauge as their southern neighbour and consequently, when the day arrived, I travelled in great comfort without having to change trains. On my arrival in Brisbane, being nearly 500 miles north of Sydney, I immediately noticed the considerable difference in temperature.

The office manager introduced me to his staff who consisted only of six people.

"Your accommodation is also arranged," he added, "I have a small self-contained guest apartment in the back of my garden which you can use. And whilst we are away you can water the flowers."

The apartment turned out to be very comfortable accommodation and within walking distance of the offices.

Whilst lacking the bustling atmosphere of the Sydney offices, the Brisbane Depot enjoyed a regular and varied clientele and serviced a large area of the interior territory.

Accompanying one of the sales representatives one day gave me the opportunity to also finally visit a settlement where the majority of the residents were native Aborigines whom I had not come across before. It was here that I bought a genuine hunting boomerang and a piece of strangely painted tree bark which I was told was used as a messaging board amongst the Aborigines. Both these pieces have stayed with me to this very day.

The staff in the office worked so competently that my presence as an interim manager seemed almost superfluous.

On my way to the office one day I noticed a poster on a billboard inviting people to visit the whaling station of Tangalooma on Moreton Island. Here was an opportunity for yet another unique experience. When I mentioned it in the office a junior clerk, who clearly knew more about whales, mentioned that the hunting season will normally come to an end in October and I should not delay my visit to Tangalooma. To my delight he offered to join me on this trip and to procure the tickets for the ferry boat.

"It is only 15 miles offshore," he added.

Before we actually reached the whaling station my fellow traveller told me, "We are in luck today, they have caught something and I reckon it will be a humpback."

And he was right. After disembarking and walking up to the main yard of the station, we saw men in thigh-high rubber boots wielding blades on long wooden poles, slicing open the body of this gigantic creature and extracting long strips of blubbery looking flesh. It was not a pretty sight. Adding to this the overpowering smell, I welcomed the call to embark again for our return to Brisbane harbour. I was quite pleased to learn later that the whaling station was eventually closed down as the whale population in the traditional hunting grounds had been severely decimated.

At the end of my managerial role in Brisbane I was quite keen to return to Sydney and to meet up again with Keith and Norma's social clique. What I had not expected was to be told that my return to the UK by sea had been cancelled and that I should return to Glasgow by air. After having built up great expectations for my voyage back, this change of plan was very disappointing.

"I know this comes as a blow to you," the manager added, "but we could probably minimise your disappointment by arranging your return with a few selected stopovers en route to London. The first such stop could be a couple of days in Hong Kong, which I have visited myself and which you will find very interesting. Think about it and we shall then have a word with BOAC as to how best they can stagger your flight back to the UK."

When I told Keith the news he seemed to think that this was a much more exciting way of returning to the UK than being cooped up in a boat, as he called it, which was only calling on a few ports on its passage. When I mentioned that I had particularly looked forward to travelling through the Suez Canal and hopefully getting a view of the Pyramids he suggested that I should simply include Cairo as one of the stopovers on my flight plan.

"If I had been given this opportunity of stopovers travelling to the UK I would also have followed the manager's suggestion to spend some time in Hong Kong and after that I would certainly have liked to see Bangkok and maybe Delhi, after which you have interesting places like Teheran and Damascus plus Cairo and possibly a stopover in Rome before finally heading for London."

Keith obviously did not miss any geography lessons at school and the way he described my possible return to the UK sounded in the end very appealing. I decided to use Keith's proposed itinerary as my final suggestion to the manager and was pleased to hear that he found the proposal very imaginative.

"With your German passport you will require a visa for your stay in Hong Kong," he added, "but in the other places on your list you will probably obtain short-term entry visas on your arrival. Just leave it to our travel agent to sort these things out."

Finally, with my passport containing visitor's visas for Hong Kong and Bangkok and the day of my departure set for 16th November, I could no longer escape the finality of my stay in this hospitable and enterprising country. Norma had organised a farewell party at her Rose Bay House and the colleagues at the office gathered at the nearby bar to share my last glass of ice-cold Australian beer with them. I felt quite nostalgic when I finally left my apartment in Vaucluse and handed the key to the tenant on the ground floor.

Chapter 13

Keith was given time off at the office to accompany me to the airport and finally after repeated promises to stay in touch I started the first lap of my journey with a four-hour flight to Darwin. If I had thought that the Brisbane area was so much hotter than Sydney, stepping off the plane here in Darwin was yet another new experience. It was a truly sweltering heat and the high humidity made it feel even worse.

The flight from Sydney to Darwin did not only bring home the enormous distances between towns and cities in this country, but thanks to a cloudless sky I also got a good view of the vast stretches of desert-like plains, intermingled with patches of forests and shrub land and even the occasional sign of human settlement and industrial activity.

Another four-hour flight finally took me to Manila where I was scheduled to spend the night before proceeding the next morning to Hong Kong. The hotel at the airport, whilst providing overnight accommodation, displayed the decided atmosphere of a night club. After my long flight, I decided to have a quick late night drink and ventured down to the smoke-filled bar area. I had just settled down on a bar stool when a girl approached me with a strap round her neck holding a large tray with American cigarettes and some other small packages on it. I had seen female cigarette vendors before, but never one like this one. She was completely naked. It made me wonder what other surprises I would encounter on my brief journey through the exotic Far East.

The onward flight to Hong Kong was much shorter and until we finally descended on our approach to the local airport, it was quite uneventful. Soon after the announcement to fasten our seatbelts, the plane seemed to be descending at such a rapid pace that it just appeared to be missing the roof tops of buildings before touching down on the runway of Taipak Airport. At that time I had no idea that this was not only a dangerously short runway but that it ended also straight in the waters of Hong Kong harbour

My pre-booked hotel was an unassuming building in a side street off Nathan Road in Kowloon. At first I did not even recognise it as a hotel, as a large room next to the reception desk showed a long table filled with rolls of cloth and some sewing machines in the background. Space was clearly at a premium in this teeming city.

I remember you saying that your visit to the famous Chinatown in San Francisco left you somewhat unimpressed. Did the Chinese culture and way of life grab your interest more now that you see it in their own homeland?

From the moment we had landed I began to feel fascinated by this place. A courteous Chinese immigration officer gave only a quick glance at my visa and in perfect English welcomed me to Hong Kong. The forecourt to the airport building was crowded with people, taxis, tricycles and also a very traditional form of transport, a few rickshaws. I was so glad that the Sydney manager had suggested this place as an extended stopover on my return to Europe. A chance of a lifetime and all I needed now was money to indulge in the plethora of fabulous goods on offer in unobtrusive stalls and also very elegant shops, lining the streets near my hotel. Could I spare enough to buy a piece of jade for Elaine?

The following day I crossed the harbour to explore the island of Victoria with its imposing buildings of banks and commercial enterprises. Billboards drew attention to dozens of attractions for tourists like myself, but unfortunately time was not on my side. In the end, a few sets of ivory chopsticks and a small piece of jade joined my baggage as a reminder of my visit to this Far Eastern jewel of the British Empire.

During my training time at the Glasgow Head Office I had heard people referring to the Coats representation in Hong Kong but I could not recall the agency's name and in any case I thought if I called on them they would merely see me as an unknown employee amongst the thousands of employees working in the Coats group of companies.

Finally, after two most stimulating days I was back at Taipak Airport on my way west to Bangkok. It was 19th November. Would any of the other places on my journey match the atmosphere of Hong Kong? Should I have taken my whole annual leave to really explore this fascinating place and then fly straight back to the UK? Too late now.

The rest of the journey began to simulate the movements of a grasshopper. After an overnight stay in Bangkok and a few hours of sightseeing, the next stop in Delhi allowed merely a few hours in the transit area of the building and in Damascus French-speaking airport staff informed me that my connecting flight to Cairo would be leaving in two hours' time. At least my programme had allowed for two full days in Cairo with pre-booked accommodation in the Sheraton Hotel. I had always been fascinated by the history of ancient Egypt and to get at least a glimpse of the Pyramids would be the realisation of a long-held dream.

I was aware that the Suez crisis in 1956 and the dispute over the control of the famous canal had led to an ongoing fractious relationship between Egypt and the UK, but since I was travelling with a German passport I did not expect any serious problems. The overall atmosphere was tense, with soldiers controlling the access to the bus waiting to take us from the airport to the city terminal.

The location of my hotel was really excellent. Right on the banks of the River Nile and within walking distance of many of the Cairo landmarks. The hotel was in a class of its own, compared with my more spartan accommodation in Hong Kong and Bangkok.

During my first foray into crowded streets, the frequent appearance of uniformed young men gave the impression of a people still living with the aftermath of the military and political upheavals four years earlier.

Late that afternoon, when trying to complete the film in my camera with a few more shots of Cairo landmarks, I experienced personally how sensitive the authorities were to the behaviour of the public. When I saw the magnificent facade of a large building in a nearby square I was convinced I had the famous Egyptian Museum in front of me.

With my camera at the ready I was suddenly grabbed from behind by two uniformed men. I was told in English to hand over my camera whereupon one of them opened the camera and unrolled the whole film in broad daylight. I felt like screaming. Not being a very regular taker of photographic pictures, the film had not only contained pictures from Hong Kong and Bangkok, but also many pictures from my time in Australia. When I asked them as to why they had done this to me, they merely answered by demanding some form of identification from me. They took a look at my passport and after a brief conversation amongst themselves handed it back to me.

"It is strictly forbidden," the English-speaking man now explained, "to take pictures of this building which is the headquarters of our police and security services. We should really arrest you but with the film destroyed we shall take this matter no further."

After this my appetite for Cairo began to wane considerably.

Back at the hotel, and still feeling very angry about the episode in the square, I browsed through a few leaflets promoting visits to the Pyramids, Nile cruises and also railway journeys to destinations up in the river valley. The man at the reception desk assured me that on a trip to Helwan I would get a good view of the Pyramids. And so I decided to make this my programme for my next and final day in Egypt.

When I eventually found my train in the crowded railway station I already began to wonder whether I had taken the right decision. Would it not have been better to have taken a taxi to visit the nearby Pyramids? But here I was now on a crowded train with standing room only amongst strange-looking people. At the first stop, not far outside Cairo, a shuffle broke out as a group of young men tried to reach the exit door of the coach. As the train began to move again I discovered to my horror that my wallet was no longer in my hip pocket. In it were not only the few Egyptian pounds I had bought at the airport, but also the remaining US dollars which had proved to be the easiest currency when travelling through different countries. After the disaster the day before, and now having become the victim of a pickpocket, my enthusiasm for things Egyptian – including the Pyramids – had taken a severe battering.

With at least the rail ticket saved in my trouser pocket, I descended at the next station and waited for nearly two hours for a return train to Cairo. Thankfully I had left my passport and travel documents in my hotel room and the room had been paid for with the original reservation. When I reported the loss of my wallet to the head receptionist I did not receive much sympathy after I had to admit to him that I had carried my wallet in an open hip pocket.

Unlike my departure from Hong Kong or even Bangkok, I felt no regrets about leaving this place. After another short stopover in Rome it felt like coming home when the plane finally landed at Heathrow Airport. A few English coins retrieved from the pockets of a jacket in my suitcase allowed me to make a brief phone call to Elaine to inform her of my scheduled arrival at Renfrew Airport After that, I was left with one single thruppence coin, the last and only surviving remnant of my originally well-stocked purse. I decided to keep it as a souvenir.

As the plane descended into Renfrew Airport I began to wonder what our reunion would be like. What news would await me at Head Office?

If my memory serves me right it must be about seven months since you last saw each other.

In fact, Joseph, it seemed a lot longer, but through our regular correspondence and Elaine's affectionate style of reporting of events in her own life, it always made me feel as if I was included in all of it.

And there she was now, looking as radiant as ever with her smartly dressed mother beside her.

Our embrace must have looked rather formal but then I knew from past encounters that in public places – and in particular at airports – Elaine did not like an excessive display of emotions. When we reached her mother's car the reception by their poodle was definitely less constrained.

It was a real feeling of homecoming, but for the rest of the day we all wrestled with the question. What will happen tomorrow when I report back to Head Office in Glasgow? Would I merely be asked to report on my visits to the USA and Australia and answer questions on my evaluation of the blister pack for possible use in Europe? And would I then be handed an airline ticket to take me back to Freiburg?

The personnel manager greeted me with his customary firm handshake and after a few casual exchanges about my just-completed trip, informed me that I was expected in the Overseas Department for the Far East.

"A room has also been reserved for you at Makerston House and when you come back tomorrow," he added, "please bring your passport with you."

It got more mysterious by the minute.

I could hardly believe it when I was told that, having obtained the agreement from the Mez AG in Freiburg, the Company wanted me to go for a limited period to Hong Kong to assist the local agent in revitalising flagging sales. I felt like receiving an early Christmas present.

From here on, events unfolded in quick succession. Briefing sessions in the Far East Department provided me with a good background of the multitude of potential outlets for our products in the Colony, consisting not only of traditional producers of men's and ladies' outerwear, but also a widespread costume jewellery business with a regular demand for beading threads. On top of this there were also the annual negotiations in Hong Kong with representatives from the People's Republic of China for large shipments of embroidery threads to their country.

To think that only a few days ago I had passed through Hong Kong, believing that I would probably never have the opportunity again to visit this place – it all seemed like a dream.

My parents did not seem too surprised when I informed

them about my new venture.

"Can we at least expect you back when you have finished your assignment in Hong Kong?" my mother asked.

I did not have an answer.

Amongst the souvenirs acquired during my just-completed journey, the little koala bear seemed to be more appreciated than anything else. It has been a family member ever since.

As to be expected during the festive days, my impending return to Hong Kong was a popular topic of conversation wherever we went, sometimes followed up with the reasonable question "Will you be posted back to Germany after your return from Hong Kong?"

Although they never mentioned it, the same question must also have been uppermost in the minds of Elaine and her mother.

Finally, with New Year's celebrations over, my passport duly filled with yet another visa for Hong Kong, the day had arrived for another farewell at Renfrew Airport. The last few weeks had brought us closer together again, but with so many questions on my future, how much longer could an exchange of letters, however frequent, keep alive the ardour of our relationship? I did not however linger on this for long as the prospect of returning to Hong Kong again began to preoccupy my mind.

When I took a closer look at my flight ticket I saw that from London onwards I would once again stop in Rome and that I would also have a full day's break in Bombay.

On 13th January 1961, the plane, just missing the

rooftops of the nearby houses again, landed at Taipak. How will the local Company agent receive me? Will I be seen as a kind of inspector to check up on them? A middle-aged Chinese gentleman was in the arrivals hall with my name on a board. He introduced himself as Mr Lu from the Davie Boag Agency and handed me a letter from the chairman in which he welcomed me to Hong Kong. He was looking forward to meeting me and agreeing a work programme for my stay in the Colony. He also added that the agency had already taken steps to secure suitable accommodation for me. Meanwhile I should stay in the hotel in Kowloon and report to the Agency Offices in Jardine House on Victoria Island the following day. It all sounded so reassuring and as it turned out, it truly was the beginning of a most memorable period of my employment with the Coats Company.

Jardine House was an impressive skyscraper, although still dwarfed by the nearby bank buildings which dominated the waterfront. Like the chairman's family who hailed from Greenock in Scotland, the majority of senior staff had a Scottish background. When I told them of my engagement to a young lady from Paisley it quickly removed any reservations they may have had about someone with a German passport being sent to them for temporary assistance.

I was delighted to hear that an apartment had been secured for me in a large building called Hacienda on the peak of Victoria Island, but instead of looking out onto Hong Kong harbour it had a southward view of the colourful township of Aberdeen.

Since it was a large double apartment with quarters for a

live-in Chinese housekeeper couple, I was told that I would have to share the accommodation with a young Englishman who was already in residence there. He also worked in Jardine House, but for a local insurance company.

It all made my past accommodations sound quite frugal. The daily trip by funicular to and from work was an additional novelty. Sharing the apartment with Ron was very much to my advantage, as he could familiarise me with all the domestic arrangements. It was a new world for me. Rising in the morning to find a lavishly prepared breakfast table, a freshly ironed shirt laid out for the day and shoes having a shine as never before. It looked like a dangerous path to getting spoilt.

In the office, Mr Lu became my mentor. He patiently explained the habits and rules of doing business with Chinese companies as he accompanied me for several days during my introductory visits to numerous enterprises on the Kowloon side of Hong Kong. I noticed from the beginning that Mr Lu spent considerable time in introducing me to the customer, but as it was all done in Cantonese I was unaware of what he said.

"They all speak English perfectly," he explained, "but I used our own language to introduce you as a special representative, sent from Scotland to meet important customers for Coats products here in Hong Kong. It will be very beneficial once you make further visits on your own in the future. I have already asked for a special visiting card to be printed for you in our two languages."

In the office, the chairman's son David, who was of my

own age, explained to me that the Chinese New Year was about to start and that staff would take a couple of days off. Would I like to join him on the family yacht for a trip round the island? You can guess my answer. Not only was it an experience of a lifetime, but also the beginning of a lasting friendship with David.

Listening to all this one begins to ask if you remembered that you had been sent there to do some serious work.

Yes, after a very noisy new year celebration and, according to the newspaper, several suicides of people who could not cope with their debts, trips on the Star Ferry to Kowloon became a daily event. My main targets were the large manufacturers of gents' shirts destined for many European markets. The factory floors dwarfed anything I had seen before. Rows and rows of young girls behind their sewing machines and others pushing large trollies through the passages carrying bales of cloth and finished products.

It was on one of those visits that I learnt a lesson which left its mark on me for the rest of my business life. As we walked through the rows of machinists, one of them suddenly complained that the Coats thread broke repeatedly on her button-holing machine. The foreman made a few adjustments to the sewing machine, but still no improvement. I had never had a complaint about this product from other customers and I asked the girl to vacate her seat and to let me try to solve the problem. With a few adjustments to a tension disk everything worked perfectly again, except that from that moment I had lost the account of this customer. I had shown up the foreman in front of all the machinists around us. It was a serious wound to his status and it took several months and intervention at the most senior management level before the account could be recovered.

The Davie Boag Agency was also the appointed agent for the much smaller Portuguese enclave of Macau only a short boat ride away from Hong Kong, but on a route continuously patrolled by coastguards of the People's Republic of China. Mr Lu had already warned me that the boat would be full of people whose only purpose on that voyage was to visit the huge casino.

"Gambling is prohibited in Hong Kong," he added, "unless you go to the Happy Valley where you can lose your money on horses."

I had no idea what to expect when I stepped off the boat. Compared with bustling Hong Kong, this place appeared almost provincial. Some of the waiting taxis looked more like vintage cars and even the men with their tricycles lacked the smart appearance of their counterparts at Taipak Airport. To my surprise, despite being a territory administered by Portugal, the traffic was on the left side of the road.

When visiting the half dozen customers on my list it soon became clear that visits from staff of the agency had been very infrequent in the past and therefore now being visited by a representative of the Scottish parent company helped considerably to secure valuable orders for our products, some of which I learnt would most likely find their way over the border into mainland China. One very soon got the impression that Macau's relationship with its Communist neighbour was decidedly less strained than what I had heard and seen in Hong Kong. The absence of a big garrison in Macau no doubt helped their big neighbour to adopt a more relaxed attitude.

Before returning to Hong Kong, I paid a brief visit to the casino, the target of so many of my co-travellers two days ago. Having seen pictures of European casinos in films and publications I expected to find something similar here. But I was about to learn something new again. The main hall was enormous and tables as far as I could see. The place was void of the baroque-like décor often typical of European casinos. It was late in the afternoon and already the hall was teeming with people crowding round tables and long queues to buy chips for the roulette tables. Judging by the scene here, the Chinese regarded gambling as a serious pastime.

Back in Hong Kong, I switched my visiting programme to customers who supplied the European markets with embroidered tablecloths, leather goods and also custom jewellery, predominantly beaded necklaces. It had never occurred to me before how much high-quality thread would be required for the mass production of necklaces. As the weeks went by I really began to feel a part of this hub of commercial activity. The staff at the Agency went out of their way to include me in their social circles and families and Mr Lu volunteered valuable advice on how to make purchases at the lowest price in a market where there was a historic pattern of different prices for tourists, European residents and the local Chinese population. As I was about to purchase a large hand-carved camphor chest for shipment to Scotland, Mr Lu's timely advice was much appreciated and I was very pleased when he volunteered to make this purchase on my behalf.

Ever since my arrival in Hong Kong the amount of incoming correspondence had decidedly increased, not only from Elaine and her mother but also from my own parents and redirected mail from Australia, sent via the Company's Glasgow Head Office. One of Elaine's letters alerted me to the fact that the daughter of a family friend, Betty MacFarlane, was the chief matron at the large hospital in Kowloon. It was quite reassuring to know that if at any time medical help was needed I could possibly benefit from such a family connection. When I telephoned Betty, she was delighted that I had made contact with her and invited me to visit her at my earliest convenience. This led to several very pleasant encounters during the rest of my stay, culminating on one occasion in a stylish afternoon tea at the Peninsula Hotel. None of us had any idea at this stage that at one day in the future her parent's home in Scotland would be the last place where I called myself a bachelor.

Only a few months earlier I had felt quite nostalgic when leaving Australia but I have to admit, now I felt even more nostalgic about leaving Hong Kong. The dreaded letter with instructions for my return to Glasgow duly arrived early May, stating that I should report back to Head Office on 5th June.

The Chinese grapevine in Hong Kong must clearly work

very efficiently, probably with the clandestine support of Mr Lu, because on 6th May an invitation landed on my desk from the Hong Kong Thread Union for an official dinner to be held on 8th May at the Kin Kwok Restaurant in Queen's Road at 8pm. I had never heard of this association before. In the office, nobody was able or willing to explain the background to this invitation, except to say that it was a very reputable restaurant.

I was truly taken aback when I arrived at the restaurant to be greeted by a large number of the customers I had visited during the last few months and several members of the Davie Boag Agency, with Mr Lu trying to hide shyly in the background. Not only was I treated to a sumptuous farewell dinner, but a story had obviously got round that I was returning to Scotland to get married. In the corner of the dining room was a low-level Chinese coffee table with traditional carvings, a wedding present from my hosts. I felt very touched by their generosity and when I explained in my thank-you speech that my wedding date had not even been fixed yet, they merely responded with a series of jocular remarks and expressed the hope that their clearly early wedding present will help to bring about the Happy Day very soon.

It was only about a week or so after this happy event that David invited me to the Boag residence for a farewell dinner. David had made plans for a visit to the UK by train. It had taken him weeks to obtain all the permits and visas for passages through numerous communist countries.

"And, with a bit of luck," he added, "I shall be in Scotland before you!"

I thought this was a fascinating adventure which I would have quite liked to have shared with him, but apart from a certain veto from the Company I was not sure if my West German passport would have received the same respectful treatment in those countries as David's British passport. Having read and heard about the turmoil in the People's Republic of China and the deprivations caused by The Great Leap Forward I was surprised that at this time foreigners could in fact still travel by train through their country.

Two or three days prior to David's invitation, local newspapers and the radio had already mentioned the possibility of a severe typhoon veering towards the Colony. It had already started to rain when I arrived at his home, but within an hour the winds had developed into a howling crescendo, with trees in the garden bending over as if they were mere blades of grass, and the rain was lashing furiously against the large main window in the sitting room. Suddenly, with a loud cracking noise, the smaller side window in the room was sucked out of its frame and shattered on the outside patio. We all retreated to the dining room at the back of the house and with everybody wondering how much more damage the unleashed elements would inflict upon the house, the meal became a rather subdued affair. I was offered to stay for the night as it had to be expected that many of the roads back to the station of the Peak Funicular had become impassable. Hong Kong had indeed been hit by one of the severest typhoons ever recorded and, as I learnt in the ensuing days, had led not only to a great deal of damage to many private and public buildings, but also to many fatalities amongst the hillside shanty settlements, many of which were washed down from their already precarious locations. 19th May certainly became a day to remember.

After another week of visits to customers in Kowloon, and also making a few more private purchases, the day of departure finally arrived. I felt envious of Ron who had a two-year contract with his employer and could continue to enjoy the comfort of the apartment in La Hacienda and be spoilt by our housekeeper couple. With a two-year contract, I thought, I might even have been able to persuade Elaine to join me.

When saying my final goodbye to all the members of the agency, I really felt I had known them for years. It was quite an emotional occasion.

David had already set off on his epic train journey back to the UK and it was Mr Lu again who escorted me back to Taipak Airport.

Chapter 14

Apart from an extended stopover in Singapore, the rest of the journey consisted of refuelling stops in Karachi and Athens with waiting times spent in transit lounges. Throughout the journey I could not stop thinking of what I had just left behind, but when I finally saw the landmarks of London below me I told myself that hankering after the past will not help in dealing with what may lay ahead.

So far I had not been able to inform Elaine about the exact details of my arrival apart from letting her know that it would be sometime on 1st June. With 1st June being a normal working day I did not expect Elaine or her mother to be at home during the afternoon and I decided to surprise them by simply arriving on their doorstep in Elderslie. The welcome by the family poodle was nearly as rapturous as that of the two ladies of the house. There was a lot to report on both sides and as to be expected the overriding question was: what will you be told on Monday at Head Office? Will there be another overseas assignment? Would I return to the Mez AG in Freiburg to fill the position I had held before?

With no answers to any of these questions, the weekend ahead seemed particularly long.

The personnel manager received me with his usual bonhomie and, without me even getting a chance to ask questions, informed me that after a week of debriefing in the Far East Department, Dr Mez was expecting me back in Freiburg. He added that they had already heard from Hong Kong that the Agency had very much appreciated my assistance and that the Far East director would like to see me before my return to Germany.

Deep down I had already expected what I had now been told, because for some time I had had the feeling that the Mez AG had only loaned me out to the Head Office in Glasgow for this short secondment to Hong Kong, as they had continued to pay my full salary into my Freiburg bank account.

In my personal life and my relationship with Elaine it all seemed like being back to square one. We were now into the third year of our engagement and still not any closer to taking our final vows together.

When I broke the news to Elaine she seemed to take it quite calmly. Was there still something I could do to make Freiburg sufficiently attractive for her to join me as my future wife?

To be very frank, Joseph, my own exposure during the last year to the wider world and different lifestyles had begun to make me see life in Freiburg with different eyes. It was a place of learning, it was orderly and sheltered with spectacular surroundings attracting tourists from many countries and yet it lacked the vibrant and liberal atmosphere of the places which I had been fortunate enough to call my temporary home during my recent past. I had to ask the question, will Freiburg be the endpoint of my professional career? With no alternative solution in sight at this moment

I needed to put my own reservations aside and see what else I could do to sell the idea of life in Germany to Elaine and, above all, secure also her mother's approval.

I wondered if a traditional German Christmas, when Freiburg provided a particularly homely and festive atmosphere, would make Elaine look more favourably upon the possibility of living there; but then I already received a strong hint, on the day of my return from Hong Kong, how much daughter and mother were looking forward to celebrating Christmas with me again in Scotland.

In the end, all I could come up with was a suggestion for Elaine to come to Freiburg for a short holiday before Christmas to practice a little skiing and for me to return to Scotland for the Christmas and new year season.

And with this rather unsatisfactory conclusion, and many other unanswered questions still in the air, on 12th June 1961 I finally set off on my journey back to Freiburg.

Although my parents and my youngest brother were clearly overjoyed to see me back, again my own reaction was noticeably muted. The motherly instinct sensed my feeling of discomfort very quickly and she asked me outright if my relationship with Elaine had suffered a setback. She now also disclosed that when, during my absence, brother Dietmar had paid a visit to Scotland, he told her on his return that Elaine had made it quite clear to him that she would never settle down in Germany.

Had you not reached a stage by now where you yourself needed to re-examine your relationship with Elaine more thoroughly and let the brain rule over your heart?

This is more easily said than done, Joseph. I had noticed no faltering in Elaine's affection for me but after my own exposure to the Anglo-Saxon way of life I was actually beginning to better understand her attitude. I have to admit I found myself in a state of turmoil and confusion, something which I had always thought only happened to other people.

Thankfully, as the weeks passed by my work at the Mez AG required my full commitment. There was also no shortage of invitations from friends and acquaintances to question me about my recent travels. On top of all this, a young man arrived one day at the office and was introduced to me as a management trainee from Scotland. His knowledge of the German language was very limited and it fell to me to be his guide and mentor. It reminded me of my own situation in 1957 when my fellow trainee, Andrew, received me at Glasgow Central Station.

Duncan was a cheerful young man for whom Germany was his first trip outside his home country. With me just having become the proud owner of a three-cylinder DKW car, Duncan was only too happy to accompany me from time to time on my weekend outings into the Black Forest and the picturesque villages of the nearby Kaiserstuhl region.

It was only a few weeks after his arrival that Duncan admitted to having made the acquaintance of a young local lady who spoke English very well. He added, however, that this was merely a friendship and that he would not allow this to develop any further.

I was once in that situation myself I told him but, as

you know, in the end fate decided differently and left me struggling ever since with seemingly insurmountable problems.

Elaine's arrival in November coincided with days of heavy snowfall in the mountains and a picturesque white dusting of the surrounding forests. As ever before our relationship was close and passionate but like the proverbial two ostriches who stick their heads into the sand we avoided getting down to seeking a solution for our future together. Elaine thoroughly enjoyed her first attempts on skis and the cosy atmosphere of the restaurants and guest houses on the Schauinsland mountains, but I felt that deep down she was really only a visiting tourist.

With Christmas only a few weeks away it was quite a casual parting at Basel Airport. On my return to Freiburg my mother started probing again if we had come to any conclusion about our future yet.

"I was only engaged to your father for six months before we married," she said.

I could understand her curiosity, but not having an answer only added to my growing irritation over her questioning.

Spending Christmas and the new year in Scotland had by now almost become the norm. I no longer felt like being in a foreign land and the thought of making it my permanent home crossed my mind from time to time. But how?

During the festive days on our customary round of visits to Elaine's wider family and friends, I had to face similar questions to those in Freiburg. When I insinuated that so far Elaine had not displayed any fervent enthusiasm for a future in Germany, some people suggested that I should simply apply for a position with the Coats Company here in Scotland.

I knew only too well from my days as a resident of Makerston House, and also from discussions with staff at the Glasgow Head Office, that all foreign trainees were earmarked for future management functions in their own overseas subsidiaries. Hence my chances of being offered a position here in Scotland or the rest of the UK was literally non-existent. Nevertheless I decided that, once back in Freiburg, I would seek some advice from my senior management and find out if they were willing to take this matter further on my behalf.

I imagine you had a rather frosty reception when you approached your manager, presumably Dr Mez himself.

It took me actually several months before I finally plucked up enough courage to explain my predicament to Dr Mez. He listened to me very calmly and as I had expected, explained to me that my extensive training had been designed to serve the Coats Group in their German subsidiary.

"I am very certain," he added, "that the Glasgow Head Office will not offer you any employment in the UK and that at best they might possibly consider you for a position in the Company's worldwide network of companies."

"It is rather strange," he went on, "that your Scottish fiancée has not taken a liking to this picturesque region of

Germany. Our resident Scottish colleague, Mr Grant and his wife have been here for years and have become very involved in our Freiburg society."

Somehow I could not bring myself round to explain to him in more detail, that unlike the Grants, my fiancée was an only child with a strong-willed widowed mother who was also continuing to run her late husband's insurance business.

In the end, Dr Mez agreed to put my case to Head Office in Glasgow, stressing again that he did not expect a quick response.

Despite these ongoing uncertainties, the correspondence between Elaine and myself flourished but I was beginning to sense that we were both resorting more and more to general news topics rather than sharing thoughts on our future. It must have been July when I learnt that Elaine and her mother had booked a holiday in Italy for the middle of August at a place called Cadenabbia on Lake Como, and that they were hoping that I could join them.

It was just a few days before I left Freiburg to join Elaine and her mother in Cadenabbia when Dr Mez called me into his office to tell me that he had had a response from Glasgow. In short, the Coats Company could not offer me any position in the United Kingdom but there was a senior vacancy in Thailand. Had I been an unattached young man, such a posting would no doubt have been welcomed with great enthusiasm, but in my circumstances it completely failed to address my problem.

On my arrival in Cadenabbia I found the reception hall of the hotel bustling with ladies and gentlemen speaking in

German. Whilst checking myself in, a bevy of people came down the central staircase and in the midst of them was a familiar figure, Herr Strauss, the ebullient defence minister of West Germany. When I finally met up with Elaine and her mother they told me that apparently several members of the West German Cabinet had been booked into the hotel.

As I had expected, my news about the possibility of a posting to Thailand was received with two gloomy faces. Maybe I should have pretended not to have had any news from Glasgow at the beginning of our holiday because it certainly cast a shadow on the few days we had together. If Germany was not a solution to solving the problem of our future, far away Thailand was clearly regarded as even less desirable. Another cul-de sac?

It must have been halfway through our holiday when Elaine made some pointed remarks about her own employer, Imperial Chemical Industries or ICI in short, who was amongst many other industrial activities also a major force in the textile sector both in the UK and internationally. If I did not object, she could have a word with her own personnel manager to find out if the textile organisation whose offices were not in Scotland but somewhere further south in England, was currently looking for qualified staff. I suddenly remembered the imposing ICI House in Melbourne. With mixed feelings I agreed that she should make some tentative enquiries on her return.

On my return to Freiburg I mentioned nothing of this to my parents. They had repeatedly expressed their pride in my career progression in the MEZ AG and still harboured the thought that in the end I might persuade Elaine to settle down in Germany. Equally they may have thought that our relationship might come to an end and that I might then decide to choose a secure future in Freiburg, the town which after all had become our new home after our escape from the GDR.

As the weeks passed by, my mind became more and more occupied with the potential consequences of Elaine's suggestion. My affinity to Freiburg had certainly lessened since my exposure to exciting cities and locations in other parts of the world, and from what I had experienced so far I was sure I would have no problems in fully adapting to an Anglo-Saxon way of life. But then there was that painful moral dilemma. Had it not been for my present and caring employer, none of those varied and exciting episodes of the recent past would have occurred. Could I now really turn my back on them?

It was early November when Elaine mentioned in her letter that her personnel manager had in fact made contact with his colleague in the ICI Fibres Division and that he had received a positive response. They were in the process of expanding their business into Continental Europe and were looking for suitable staff for their Export Department, located in a town called Harrogate in the county of Yorkshire. If I were interested I was to try to come early for the Christmas break and she would ask her manager to arrange for me to present myself personally to the people in Harrogate.

You must have rejoiced when reading this encouraging news.

Possibilities now seem to turn into probabilities and there is at long last some light at the end of the tunnel.

Yes, Joseph, it was indeed tremendous news, but it did not remove my moral dilemma regarding my current employer where, after all my training, I now had good prospects for an early progression into senior management. With a new employer I would no doubt have to start again at the bottom of the ranking order. It certainly felt I had reached a crossroad now. The challenge of the unknown brought back memories of my childhood days when I ventured across the Iron Curtain border, depending a great deal on good luck and often unexpected help from selfless strangers.

With all that in mind I informed Elaine that I would be delighted to take this matter further and if an interview could be arranged before Christmas I would plan my arrival in Scotland accordingly.

In her next letter, Elaine informed me that the people in Harrogate had agreed to see me before Christmas. On 18th December1962 I once again set off on what by now had almost become a routine flight to Glasgow and only two days later I found myself on a five-hour train journey to Harrogate.

My immediate impression was very positive. Elegant shops, large houses with well-tended gardens and wide tree-lined open parklike spaces created the atmosphere of a very prosperous town. This initial favourable impression was further enhanced when I finally reached my destination, the headquarters of the ICI Fibres Division in Hookstone Road.

An impressive complex of modern buildings, but no sign of any factories or large warehouse buildings. It clearly was the administrative heart of this organisation.

My interview with the export manager turned out to be a rather casual affair. After a brief description of my own background, which, judging by his facial expression caught his full attention, he explained the role which ICI, as the inventor of the polyester fibre, occupies internationally and how with the upcoming expiry of patent rights, the Company now needed to strengthen its own commercial presence in many overseas markets. And in this context, one of the main areas of the world was Continental Europe

Finally he asked me for my private address in Freiburg and suggested that I now send a written request for employment in the Company's Fibres Division to the Central Personnel Department at the ICI Headquarters in London. I was not sure whether this was an indication that my interview with him had been successful or whether he was merely using the London department as a means of letting me know that I had failed. I was pleased when he offered me a Company chauffeured car to take me back to the station to catch my afternoon train back to Glasgow.

As to be expected, the visit to Harrogate became the main theme for the rest of my Christmas break. I could already detect in the way Elaine was talking to her mother that my acceptance in Harrogate would be just a matter of formalities and that our future in the UK was now a forgone conclusion. The fact that I had received not even the slightest indication of the type of position they may offer made me dampen their enthusiasm with some words of caution. To Elaine and her mother however, over three years of uncertainties and indecisions and a relationship kept alive mainly by correspondence was now at long last coming to an end and, above all, on their terms.

It must have given you quite a strange feeling when you returned to your workplace in Freiburg. And then there were your parents. What was their reaction?

Strangely enough, my mother did not seem to be too surprised. With the proverbial instinct, attributed to mothers generally, she must have sensed for some time, that I was getting restless over my inability to find a solution to my future with Elaine, and with my brother Lothar also having left home to start a new life in South Africa, she knew that wanderlust was part of our family make up.

In the office, and also opposite Duncan, I remained tight lipped over my latest visit to Scotland. As a camouflage I immersed myself in my work with extra fervour. It took me the best part of two days to write my letter of application naming both the MEZ AG in Freiburg and the parent company J. & P. Coats in Glasgow for references.

It was only a week later when a letter arrived from London to acknowledge the receipt of my application and that it was receiving their attention. At least not an outright rejection.

From here onwards it all developed quickly into an unstoppable sequence of joyful and also sad events. At the end of April I received the confirmation that ICI had received a reference from J. & P. Coats on the basis of which they were now offering me a position in the Export Department of their Fibres Division in Harrogate, starting on 1st July 1963, with a salary of £1,400 per annum.

It was several years later that I obtained a copy of a letter from the Personnel Department in Glasgow to ICI, dated 29th May 1963 which I should read out to you as it describes in a few words the end of a long journey which not so long ago seemed like a journey to nowhere.

Dear Rory,

Thank you for your telephone call and subsequent letter of 27th May about Wolfgang Pietrek. I enclose an official reference which I hope will do. We think a lot of him here, but I fear the girl from Elderslie has been too much for his career ambitions in our business. She also, I believe, has a mother — and it takes a strong man to stand up to a really determined mother-in law elect!

Will hope to see you again sometime soon.
Yours
Robin.

With a firm offer of employment from ICI, the most dreaded moment had now arrived. To hand in my resignation to my present employer. No doubt they would express their deep disappointment in me after all the opportunities they had given me over the years, but to my great relief the general manager received my news calmly and without any sign of reproach or resentment. The Glasgow Head Office had already informed them about the request from ICI for a reference and my announcement therefore did not come as a surprise. The fact, however, that Dr Mez himself did not want to see me before my departure was an indication that my sudden resignation was after all regarded as an act of ingratitude. My announcement caused considerable consternation and questioning amongst my colleagues, but both Duncan and the resident Scottish manager, Mr Grant, wished me good luck for a happy future in their own country. It was a strange feeling of embarrassment and guilt when I passed the Concierge's little office for the last time and he smilingly greeted me with *"Auf Wiedersehen"*.

At home, my mother had already gone into overdrive to assemble all the things she thought I needed for my new life abroad. The garage where I had originally bought my DKW gave the car a thorough check-up and, after bidding my farewell to old friends from school and college and the European Youth Movement, the moment had finally arrived to say goodbye to my parents and my brother Dietmar. During all those years, saying goodbye had almost become a routine event in our family, but this time we all knew it was a historic and life-changing moment.

It was Monday 23rd June when I finally headed for the motorway to Strasbourg, after having made a brief stop at the Freiburg Minster and also having a last nostalgic look at my old school, the Rotteck Gymnasium and the University opposite.

Driving through Strasbourg brought back memories of my first visit to this city with my friend Gert on our hired 125 cc Wanderer motorbike.

My original plan was to stop in Paris for a couple of days before proceeding to Calais, but casting my mind back to the frantic traffic during my earlier visit to this metropolis I decided that it was best not to expose my car and also myself to any possibility of an accident which could result in dire consequences for my onward journey. After a night in a comfortable little roadside hotel on the eastern outskirts of Paris, I set off early in the morning for the final stretch to Calais.

It was a very different scene compared with my very first Channel crossing in April 1957. On wide modern roads flanked by large signposts, a stream of cars and lorries were heading towards the port area, where in the distance I could already see the upper structure of a large ship. With no firm pre-booking for my crossing I was asked to wait in a large car park right at the waterfront. The official, however, assured me that once the loading of the existing firm bookings was completed that they would still find space for my little DKW.

And so, on 24th June 1963, seven years after my first departure from Calais, I drove my car over a creaky ramp into the gaping rear opening of a P&O ferry taking me to the land where at long last Elaine and I could build our future together.

Was it a dream come true and the end of an often-bewildering journey?

Or was it merely the beginning of yet another journey into the unknown?